New Da

G000144846

Edited by **Sally Welch** January–April 2022

15 The Chambers, Vineyard
Abingdon OX14 3FE
brf.org.uk

Bible Reading Fellowship is a charity (233280)
and company limited by guarantee (301324),
registered in England and Wales

ISBN 978 1 80039 124 6

Cover image © Chinnapong/stock.adobe.com;
illustration on p. 143 © bernardojbp/stock.adobe.com

Distributed in Australia by:
MediaCom Education Inc, PO Box 610, Unley, SA 5061
Tel: 1 800 811 311 | admin@mediacom.org.au

Distributed in New Zealand by:
Scripture Union Wholesale, PO Box 760, Wellington 6140
Tel: 04 385 0421 | suwholesale@clear.net.nz

Acknowledgements
Scripture quotations marked with the following abbreviations are taken from the
version shown. **NRSV:** The New Revised Standard Version of the Bible, Anglicised
Edition, copyright © 1989, 1995 by the Division of Christian Education of the
National Council of the Churches of Christ in the USA. Used by permission. All
rights reserved. **NIV:** The Holy Bible, New International Version, Anglicised edition,
copyright © 1979, 1984, 2011 by Biblica. Used by permission of Hodder & Stoughton
Publishers, an Hachette UK company. All rights reserved. 'NIV' is a registered
trademark of Biblica. UK trademark number 1448790. **GNT:** The Good News Bible
published by The Bible Societies/HarperCollins Publishers Ltd, UK © American
Bible Society 1966, 1971, 1976, 1992, used with permission. **MSG:** The Message,
copyright © 1993, 1994, 1995, 1996, 2000, 2001, 2002 by Eugene H. Peterson. Used
by permission of NavPress. All rights reserved. Represented by Tyndale House
Publishers, Inc. NKJV: The New King James Version®. Copyright © 1982 by Thomas
Nelson. Used by permission. All rights reserved. **NIRV:** The Holy Bible,
New International Reader's Version®. Copyright © 1996, 1998 Biblica. All rights
reserved throughout the world. Used by permission of Biblica.

'Anna' by Nicola Slee (pp. 19, 20, 22) copyright © Nicola Slee 2007. Reproduced
from *The Book of Mary* with permission of SPCK through PLSclear.

Reflection by Margaret Silf (p. 15) copyright © Margaret Silf 2020.

A catalogue record for this book is available from the British Library

Printed by Gutenberg Press, Tarxien, Malta

Suggestions for using *New Daylight*

Find a regular time and place, if possible, where you can read and pray undisturbed. Before you begin, take time to be still and perhaps use one of the BRF prayers on page 6. Then read the Bible passage slowly (try reading it aloud if you find it over-familiar), followed by the comment. You can also use *New Daylight* for group study and discussion, if you prefer.

The prayer or point for reflection can be a starting point for your own meditation and prayer. Many people like to keep a journal to record their thoughts about a Bible passage and items for prayer. In *New Daylight* we also note the Sundays and some special festivals from the church calendar, to keep in step with the Christian year.

New Daylight and the Bible

New Daylight contributors use a range of Bible versions, and you will find a list of the versions used opposite. You are welcome to use your own preferred version alongside the passage printed in the notes. This can be particularly helpful if the Bible text has been abridged.

New Daylight affirms that the whole of the Bible is God's revelation to us, and we should read, reflect on and learn from every part of both Old and New Testaments. Usually the printed comment presents a straightforward 'thought for the day', but sometimes it may also raise questions rather than simply providing answers, as we wrestle with some of the more difficult passages of scripture.

New Daylight is also available in a deluxe edition (larger format). Visit your local Christian bookshop or BRF's online shop **brfonline.org.uk**. To obtain an audio version for the blind or partially sighted, contact Torch Trust for the Blind, Torch House, Torch Way, Northampton Road, Market Harborough LE16 9HL; +44 (0)1858 438260; **info@torchtrust.org**.

Comment on *New Daylight*

To send feedback, please email **enquiries@brf.org.uk**, phone **+44 (0)1865 319700** or write to the address shown opposite.

Writers in this issue

Gordon Giles is canon chancellor of Rochester Cathedral. Married with a teenage daughter, he was previously a vicar in north London and was also responsible for training junior clergy. He has written various devotional books published by BRF and also SPCK, on church music and hymnody.

Paul Gravelle is an Anglican priest in Auckland, New Zealand. He is a poet, writer and retreat leader and has ministered in military, urban and rural settings, supporting himself as an industrial journalist.

Terry Hinks is a United Reformed Church minister, serving two churches in the High Wycombe area. His special interests are Christian unity, community engagement and the care of God's creation, alongside a deep love of the Bible, stillness and prayer.

Liz Hoare is an ordained Anglican priest and teaches spiritual formation at Wycliffe Hall, Oxford. Her interests lie in the history and literature of Christian spirituality and their connections with today's world. She is married to Toddy, a priest and sculptor, and they have a teenage son.

Andy John is the bishop of Bangor and has served there for more than a decade, with all his ministry having been spent in the Church in Wales. Apart from being a bishop, he occasionally attempts marathons (Snowdonia being a favourite) and enjoys time with his now grown-up children.

Margaret Silf is an ecumenical Christian committed to working across and beyond traditional divisions. She is the author of a number of books for 21st-century spiritual pilgrims and a retreat facilitator. She is a mother and grandmother and lives in North Staffordshire.

Fiona Stratta worked as a speech and language therapist, and now works as a tutor and speech and drama teacher. She is author of *Walking with Gospel Women* and *Walking with Biblical Women of Courage*, both published by BRF.

Debbie Thrower is a former broadcaster and has pioneered Anna Chaplaincy for Older People in Alton, Hampshire, since 2010 – joining BRF in 2014. She's an Anglican licensed lay minister and has a daughter, a son and a two-year-old granddaughter.

Sally Welch writes...

Whenever I am stuck for ideas or inspiration for a sermon, I go for a walk. My favourite walk in these situations goes between my two churches – a round trip of about five miles. As you can imagine, I have walked the path frequently. The route is always the same, the landscape never changes – the hills, the forest, the achingly beautiful view of fields and villages, gentle hills and the occasional sight of the river. And yet the walk is always different. It's different because of the seasons, adding tone and depth to the perpetual landscape. It's different because of who I am when I walk it, the mood I am in, the experiences I am having. Always the same, always new.

The stories of our faith are similar to that walk – always the same, always new. Hefting is a traditional method of managing flocks of sheep on large areas of common land and communal grazing. Initially, sheep have to be kept in an unfenced area of land by constant shepherding. Over time this becomes learned behaviour, as lambs graze with their mothers on the land, instilling a lifelong knowledge of where optimal grazing and shelter can be found throughout the year. The contents of the Bible are hefted to our memory, our imagination, our very being. They are unchanging and yet ever-changing, part of the soul story of our lives. Just as different aspects of a familiar landscape strike us each time we walk it, so do different parts of the story of salvation have an impact on us at different times in our lives, resonating with our experience, shining a new light on the way things are.

One hundred years ago, in a church in south London, The Fellowship of St Matthew was begun in response to a congregation's eagerness for informed and helpful support in building a habit of daily Bible reading. In 1926, it became known as the Bible Reading Fellowship (BRF) as its influence spread and more church communities subscribed to the notes and prayers which were offered. Today, BRF resources people and groups as they grow in faith, encouraging them to deepen their relationship with God and to share the good news of Jesus Christ with others. BRF's theme for this centenary year is 'Sharing the Story' (please see page 160 to find out more). Within the three issues of *New Daylight* this year, we will be celebrating God's story through looking back in thankfulness, 'standing still' to enjoy the present and looking forward in hope.

Sally Ann Welch

The BRF Prayer

Almighty God,
you have taught us that your word is a lamp for our feet
and a light for our path. Help us, and all who prayerfully
read your word, to deepen our fellowship with you
and with each other through your love.
And in so doing may we come to know you more fully,
love you more truly, and follow more faithfully
in the steps of your Son Jesus Christ, who lives and reigns
with you and the Holy Spirit, one God forevermore.
Amen

The BRF Centenary Prayer

Gracious God,
we rejoice in this centenary year
that you have grown BRF
from a local network of Bible readers
into a worldwide family of ministries.
Thank you for your faithfulness
in nurturing small beginnings
into surprising blessings.
We rejoice that, from the youngest to the oldest,
so many have encountered your word
and grown as disciples of Christ.
Keep us humble in your service,
ambitious for your glory
and open to new opportunities.
For your name's sake
Amen

Looking back

Should auld acquaintance be forgot,
and never brought to mind?
Should auld acquaintance be forgot,
and auld lang syne?

 So runs the first verse of that most famous song by Robert Burns, whose chorus is belted out at midnight on New Year's Eve in so many venues and is frequently sung at other times as well: graduations, stag parties, leaving events – any occasion when people gather together to mark a change in situation or status. As well as looking forward to the new, there are moments of regret and farewell for past events, and a determination to hold on to the happy memories of former times.

I must admit to mixed feelings about looking back. I am not a great one for dwelling on the past, preferring to look forward to an improved future rather than agonise over the mistakes of latter years. However, if we are to avoid making those same mistakes again, we must reflect on events gone by and learn from them. Only then will the pain of wrong choices not have been in vain. Similarly, memories of happy times and joyful events will buoy us up as we look towards an unknown future, keeping close those friends, wisdoms and experiences which help us maintain an optimistic outlook.

The Bible is not silent on the act of looking back – and as usual offers a wealth of different views on the subject. Looking back can be dangerous, even life-threatening, as Lot's wife discovers. It can be an act of disobedience, demonstrating a lack of faith in God and a disregard for his good purposes. But it can also help us to understand the reasons for our behaviour, and root us in the tradition of God's love and care for us, spreading back through generations, reinforced by covenant, demonstrated fully and finally by the sending of his Son.

So, as we begin the New Year, 'lying open before us', with its promise and possibilities, let us pause and look back, not just over the last year but over our whole lives. Thus may we better perceive the golden thread of God's love running richly through our lives, in order that it may better guide us as we journey on.

SALLY WELCH

Don't look back!

When they had brought them outside, they said, 'Flee for your life; do not look back or stop anywhere in the Plain; flee to the hills, or else you will be consumed'... Then the Lord rained on Sodom and Gomorrah sulphur and fire from the Lord out of heaven; and he overthrew those cities, and all the Plain, and all the inhabitants of the cities, and what grew on the ground. But Lot's wife, behind him, looked back, and she became a pillar of salt.

Lot's wife had it all going for her. She was the wife of a wealthy man, so she had physical comforts. Her husband was a religious man, a man of great faith, so she did not have the challenge of trying to live a good life in the face of opposition from those around her. She had been warned of the danger to her life and that of those she loved and she had set out with them to Zoar, the city which they had been guaranteed would provide safety.

Yet at the last minute, she looked back. At the last moment, she felt a sudden rush of longing for what she was leaving behind. Yes, Sodom was sinful and depraved, wicked and debauched, but still, it was what she knew. She was familiar with its ways and must surely have benefited from its luxury and ease. That one instant of regret led to her downfall. 'Remember Lot's wife,' thunders Jesus (Luke 17:32), as he urges his disciples to take seriously the coming of the kingdom.

It is easy to have a cynical and jaded approach to New Year's resolutions. After all, they are so earnestly made and so easily broken! Yet there is something to be said for using today to put behind us bad habits, destructive ways of living and being, and loveless attitudes and actions. We may well fail, we may well cast longing glances behind us, but if we call upon him, Jesus will always catch us as we fall, helping us back on our feet and turning our faces in the true direction.

Heavenly Father, protect me from falling back into habits
that you have called me to leave behind.

SALLY WELCH

The good old days?

As Pharaoh drew near, the Israelites looked back, and there were the Egyptians advancing on them. In great fear the Israelites cried out to the Lord. They said to Moses, 'Was it because there were no graves in Egypt that you have taken us away to die in the wilderness? What have you done to us, bringing us out of Egypt? Is this not the very thing we told you in Egypt, "Let us alone and let us serve the Egyptians"? For it would have been better for us to serve the Egyptians than to die in the wilderness.' But Moses said to the people, 'Do not be afraid, stand firm, and see the deliverance that the Lord will accomplish for you today; for the Egyptians whom you see today you shall never see again. The Lord will fight for you, and you have only to keep still.'

Unbelievable! Have the Israelites forgotten what it was like in Egypt? 'They made their lives bitter with harsh labour in brick and mortar and with all kinds of work in the fields; in all their harsh labour, the Egyptians worked them ruthlessly,' we are told (Exodus 1:14, NIV). And that's before their infant sons were slaughtered to try to keep the numbers down!

But things have not gone smoothly since that heady, night-time flight from Egypt. The Israelites have wandered in the desert, and now the Egyptians are after them. In their fear, they look back upon their previous situation, and instead of seeing back-breaking labour, they see security; instead of the murder of their babies, they see the certainty of settled lives. So too do we, in times of upheaval and change, long for the familiar daily round, however difficult and challenging our circumstances. 'Better the devil you know,' we might say to ourselves, and thus effectively put a stop to growth, development and moving forward in whatever aspect of our lives we are too afraid or too indolent to change.

'Do not be afraid, stand firm,' Moses exhorts his people, and us too, as we place our faith in all that God will accomplish for us today, should we only let him.

Lord, as you fight for me, help me to believe in you.

SALLY WELCH

Unfit for the kingdom

To another he said, 'Follow me.' But he said, 'Lord, first let me go and bury my father.' But Jesus said to him, 'Let the dead bury their own dead; but as for you, go and proclaim the kingdom of God.' Another said, 'I will follow you, Lord; but let me first say farewell to those at my home.' Jesus said to him, 'No one who puts a hand to the plough and looks back is fit for the kingdom of God.'

Our youngest son has a motorbike. This fills my heart with fear – every time I wave him goodbye, I pray for his safety, aware that the incidence of accidents is very high among young motorcyclists.

My anxiety is not helped by the reports he gives of his adventures on the roads – the story about Lara, for instance, the young motorist who was so surprised by James' overtaking that as she looked at him, she swerved into him. It's a natural instinct to steer towards that which you are looking at, but a dangerous one in a driver.

So Jesus tells us that whatever the direction we are looking in, our attention will be drawn towards it. In the case of a man ploughing, an uneven furrow which is difficult to sow and reap will result; in the case of a motorist, an accident; in the case of a wistful glance towards a previously damaging lifestyle, further damage to body and soul.

The decision to follow Christ should not be made lightly, but once it has been made it needs to be wholeheartedly embraced. There will be moments of doubt, dark times when belief is hard, when everything seems to speak against our choice of pathway through life. But we must not look back, accepting the crooked furrow of regret for former times. Rather, we turn to our task and, looking ahead, watch for a glimpse of the coming kingdom, which is already lighting up the horizon.

Hold on, hold on, my brother, hold on,
Hold on till the prize is won;
Hold on to the plow,
And weary not now,
For the work is almost done.
(John P. Ellis, 1820–96)

SALLY WELCH

Who do you think you are?

Abraham was the father of Isaac, and Isaac the father of Jacob, and Jacob the father of Judah and his brothers, and Judah the father of Perez and Zerah by Tamar, and Perez the father of Hezron, and Hezron the father of Aram... and Jesse the father of King David. And David was the father of Solomon by the wife of Uriah... and Jacob the father of Joseph the husband of Mary, of whom Jesus was born, who is called the Messiah.

One of my daughter's friends is a genealogist and offered to research her family tree as a wedding present. There was that sense of excitement and anticipation – perhaps one of the branches was related to someone famous or royal. But, no, diligent research offered nothing interesting, simply a long line of maltsters on one side and plasterers on the other – and one 'paper hanger'. They lived ordinary lives, and little is known about them. But without them, my daughter would not be here, nor would the joy and love which she has brought into the world.

By beginning his gospel with a genealogy, Matthew was concerned to show how Jesus was truly a child of Israel, heir to the promise as well as fulfilment of the prophecy. This is an illustrious list, including as it does kings and princes, leaders and governors. But in among those well-known names are others less familiar. Very little is known about some of them, but they too played their part in the golden thread linking Abraham, father of Israel, to Jesus, son of God.

It is easy to feel that in the great scheme of things, we do not matter much as individuals. Our joys and sorrows, loves and aspirations are but tiny flames that flicker for an instant and then are gone. But Christianity teaches us that everyone matters – that the flame of faith and love, however briefly it shines, will not only illuminate the darkness but can be handed on down the generations, providing an eternal source of hope and light.

Father of all creation, help me to be a light to those around me, so that your love can be seen to shine.

SALLY WELCH

A promise kept

Then his father Zechariah was filled with the Holy Spirit and spoke this prophecy: 'Blessed be the Lord God of Israel, for he has looked favourably on his people and redeemed them. He has raised up a mighty saviour for us in the house of his servant David, as he spoke through the mouth of his holy prophets from of old, that we would be saved from our enemies and from the hand of all who hate us.'

What an outpouring of joy and delight there is in this poem! Zechariah has been mute for the period of his wife's pregnancy and now, tongue finally loosened, he can put into words the fruit of his reflections during the time of his enforced silence. What was the sin for which the punishment was loss of speech? Disbelief – refusal to accept his part in God's work of redemption by acknowledging God's power at work within his family.

Zechariah, who, as part of the chosen tribe of priests and spiritual leaders of the children of Israel, should have known better, couldn't step out of his experience of reality into the realm of faith. He couldn't look back at God's promises, affirmed again and again through the mouths of the prophets, and take hold of the fact that through him another step would be taken towards the fulfilment of this promise. His son, longed for until his parents had given up hope of ever having offspring, would play a vital part in 'making ready a people prepared for the Lord' – and Zechariah needed to acknowledge that. He couldn't do this straight away and so was compelled into a time of reflection and prayer. Only then could he step forward into the future.

Sometimes we need to look back before we can step forward. It might be that we must reflect on what has gone by, to understand it, perhaps, or to put aside its burdens. It might be that we take comfort from the past as we wait for a resolution of our current situation, looking forward to a better future. But always we can be sure that God accompanies us as we reflect and pray.

'Guard me as the apple of the eye; hide me in the shadow of your wings'
(Psalm 17:8).

SALLY WELCH

Look back and remember

But take care and watch yourselves closely, so as neither to forget the things that your eyes have seen nor to let them slip from your mind all the days of your life; make them known to your children and your children's children.

The church I currently work with is adamant that the story of the wise men should not be swept up into the nativity story but should be separated out and given its proper place in the church calendar. So the visit of wise men from the east, who arrive sometime after the birth of Jesus and make the mistake of alerting Herod to the possibility of a contender for his power, is given its due importance. But after 20 years of Epiphany services, it is quite daunting to think up new ways of telling the story. I have told it from the point of view of the wise men, their families, the fourth wise man – even the camels who accompanied them! But even though I and a large part of my congregation mentally roll our eyes at the thought of singing 'We three kings' one more time, still the story must be told. For it is an important part of the Christian faith, these strangers and Gentiles who acknowledged Jesus as the Messiah, these people prepared to suffer no small discomfort in order to witness and worship the salvation of the human race.

Besides, although the same story is told, the context is never the same, for we change year by year. Faces, situations, whole communities are not the same as they were the last time the story was heard, so different aspects of the event gain or lose significance and must be reflected upon. And most importantly of all, every year there will be people who hear the story for the first time. Our children and our children's children must hear and wonder at the star, the journey, the gifts and the danger. Each generation must pass on the message to the next, so that the links in the chain of the revelation of God's love are never broken.

Tell me the old, old story, tell me the old, old story,
tell me the old, old story, of Jesus and his love.
(Kate Hankey, 1834–1911)

SALLY WELCH

Receiving and handing on

For I received from the Lord what I also handed on to you, that the Lord Jesus on the night when he was betrayed took a loaf of bread, and when he had given thanks, he broke it and said, 'This is my body that is for you. Do this in remembrance of me.' In the same way he took the cup also, after supper, saying, 'This cup is the new covenant in my blood. Do this, as often as you drink it, in remembrance of me.' For as often as you eat this bread and drink the cup, you proclaim the Lord's death until he comes.

How many of us really understand the mystery of the Eucharist? In my years of leading confirmation classes for both children and adults, I have tried all sorts of different ways to communicate the importance of this act and still at times find myself wondering whether I have grasped its meaning in any way. But despite the confusion and the lack of understanding, always I hold on to two things.

First, that Jesus told us to do this, therefore this is what we must do, wherever we are and whatever situation we find ourselves in. I have celebrated the last supper in fields and in houses, in churches and in cathedrals, many hundreds of times. Each time is different; every time is special. Sometimes I do not feel holy or particularly well prepared – I may be unwell or tired, dispirited or grief-stricken.

But this is where the second principle comes in – the efficacious nature of the Eucharist. That is, the fact that the sacrament is a means of divine grace does not depend on the worthiness of the person administering it. We are all sinners; we can all be redeemed through Christ's saving action on the cross. Celebrating Holy Communion together reminds us of this fact and emphasises God's grace and our forgiven status. Hallelujah!

Exalted manna, gladness of the best,
Heaven in ordinary, man well drest,
The milky way, the bird of Paradise,
Church-bells beyond the stars heard, the soul's blood,
The land of spices; something understood.
(George Herbert, 1593–1633)

SALLY WELCH

Looking back, looking forward

They shall live in the land that I gave to my servant Jacob, in which your ancestors lived; they and their children and their children's children shall live there forever; and my servant David shall be their prince forever. I will make a covenant of peace with them; it shall be an everlasting covenant with them; and I will bless them and multiply them, and will set my sanctuary among them forevermore. My dwelling-place shall be with them; and I will be their God, and they shall be my people.

What a beautiful poem of promise this is! Written by the prophet in exile, after the fall of Jerusalem, when the children of Israel have been slaughtered or captured and taken to Babylon, there is held out a picture of hope. Ezekiel reminds his people that God has never forsaken them, that he has always been faithful. If the people will only believe in the promise, and trust in God's love for them, they will once more find themselves in the land which was given to their ancestors. Not only they will live there, but their children and their children's children will too.

As I write this, we are still gripped by coronavirus – I hope that as you read this it will not still be so. Practical actions are all in place – masks, targeted lockdowns, limited social interactions, vaccinations; there is nothing further I can do. But in this helplessness lies a greater danger – that the hopelessness of the situation will overwhelm us all and we will give in to despair.

The children of Israel, exiled in Babylon, must have felt similarly threatened, so Ezekiel urges them to hope and to pray. We too can hope, and we can pray, in whatever situation we find ourselves. We can look back and remember what God has done for us in the past, and we can believe in a future which contains the same all-loving, all-caring God, whose purposes for me are good.

Look back and remember: he was with you
Stand still and realise: he is with you
Walk forward and trust: he will be with you always.
(Margaret Silf)

SALLY WELCH

Learning from Simeon and Anna

 Over the past decade or so I've had good cause to reflect on the story of Simeon and Anna. Our Anna Chaplaincy approach to supporting older people (**annachaplaincy.org.uk**), focusing on the importance of the story of one's life, is named after the widow in the second chapter of Luke's gospel.

There are many reasons why the 84-year-old woman we meet in the temple with Simeon is an inspiration for this form of ministry among men and women in their later years and their carers. Simeon and Anna are great role models of faithful older people. We're told Anna was steeped in the disciplines of fasting and prayer. We know she'd found a new way of life in the temple in her old age, one which was transformative. Together, she and Simeon are sufficiently perceptive to recognise that the young couple who brought in their baby that day for the customary rite of purification following a birth are none other than the parents of the long-hoped-for Messiah.

Luke's gospel tells us she was of the tribe of Asher. Simeon might well have been a Levite. Jews of the time would realise Anna and Simeon were poles apart socially, low and high on the 'class' spectrum, respectively. The gospel writer wished all manner of people to be able to identify with these elderly agents of God's redemptive work, who came from very different backgrounds in terms of the twelve tribes of Israel.

Today's Anna Chaplains, many of them in the older age bracket themselves with time to offer post-retirement, minister to people of strong, little or no faith at all. They're Christian chaplains but they offer spiritual and emotional care (and religious care when and where appropriate) to men and women of any and every walk of life. They're motivated by their faith to draw alongside people in their communities irrespective of whether someone has a professed faith or not.

Luke's narrative inspires Christian service today. The story of Simeon and Anna's encounter with Mary holding her new baby challenges us; it goads us in our contemporary settings, just as much as it did those in the temple precincts, to listen to Anna as she steps forward to 'speak about the child to all who were looking for the redemption of Jerusalem' (Luke 2:38, NRSV).

DEBBIE THROWER

Role models for later life

Now there was a man in Jerusalem whose name was Simeon; this man was righteous and devout, looking forward to the consolation of Israel, and the Holy Spirit rested on him.

By temperament some of us are more oriented towards the past, looking back with nostalgia, and perhaps regret, or just out of preference to thoughts of the present, let alone what lies ahead. Others of us choose to draw a line under what's happened and remain resolutely looking forward. I wonder, which are you?

Luke's gospel looks back to the events of Jesus' life but looks forward to God's salvation. The gospel writer is recording the life of Jesus to ensure the reader sees this one man as a 'Saviour, who is the Messiah, the Lord' (2:11). Despite his intention to write an 'orderly account' so 'that you may know the truth' (1:1, 4) – building on the work of eyewitnesses and ministers of the word – the author still has an agenda. He is both a historian, accurately recording past events, and a theologian, presenting them in the light of the one he has come to regard as God-sent, a Saviour, bringing salvation to the whole world.

In the second chapter of Luke we meet two older people. At least, we assume so. One of them, Anna, is a long-widowed woman of 84. About her we have a few salient details, but the profile of Simeon is puzzlingly sparse. He sounds like a man nearing the end of his life with some contentment. His wait for a glimpse of the promised Messiah has been fulfilled. But of his precise age we remain ignorant.

They are good role models for later life. Each was prayerful, expectant and, above all, hopeful. We foster resilience in the now by recalling times past, occasions when we have coped, even triumphed, despite adversity. Looking back is important if we are to welcome all that God has yet in store.

God in the now prepares us for the future. The end is not yet; with him it's just begun.

Lord, strengthen me with your blessing
and teach me to live with eternity in view.

DEBBIE THROWER

Looking forward

It had been revealed to him by the Holy Spirit that he would not see death before he had seen the Lord's Messiah.

Luke, the physician, paints a portrait of a man in which the important details are not age or hair colour but his location and his qualities. Simeon is to be found in the temple in Jerusalem. He is a worshipping man of impeccable character. What's more, Simeon is confident that God will act, and what animates Simeon is none other than the Holy Spirit, God's indwelling Spirit.

Such characteristics might not have been widely shared, one imagines, given the historical context. This was life under an occupying force, with one faction after another jockeying for power based on the claims of would-be messianic leaders. Simeon stands head and shoulders above his contemporaries, according to Luke, who sees him as favoured by God and with an instinctive eye for who's who in a crowd. He has waited patiently all these years and is on the brink of recognising something different about one young couple making their way towards him, bringing their infant to the temple for the necessary rites.

Simeon is looking forward even when the times are not propitious. The prize was to be the consolation of Israel. And not just Israel, as we shall find out. Prophetically, Simeon and Anna are the people who witness Jesus being dedicated to God by his parents, in accordance with Jewish tradition, and who recognise his uniqueness.

As a child I was a fan of the TV game show *Take Your Pick*. Would a contestant, answering a question correctly, choose to take the money or 'open the box'? Sometimes they cautiously opted for the money and one never knew what might have awaited them inside the box. Was it a consolation prize, a booby prize or a dream holiday far more valuable than the cash prize on offer? We all vacillate over choices, few more life-changing than whether we choose to face the future with confidence or with dread.

Simeon chose to be hopeful, based on the validity of God's promises in the past which had held true. Can you look forward with such confidence?

Lord, give me hope in my heart, keep me hoping.

DEBBIE THROWER

Lectio divina

Guided by the Spirit, Simeon came into the temple; and when the parents brought in the child Jesus, to do for him what was customary under the law, Simeon took him in his arms and praised God.

I once used the story of Simeon and Anna as the passage for a group of people on retreat to practise *lectio divina* on – reading slowly, bringing all our gifts of imagination to bear on the words of scripture and harnessing our senses to place ourselves in touching distance of the sights, sounds and smells of a hot day with crowds pressing into the temple courts.

Those who took part in the exercise described vivid images of cooing doves, sweaty bodies, dust motes in the glare of shafts of sunlight and pillars casting deep shadows. This was where these two elderly people spent so many of their days and, in Anna's case, nights, perhaps hunkering down with only a woollen cloak wrapped round her old bones for warmth.

Lectio divina, a traditional monastic practice of scriptural reading, meditation and prayer, is intended to promote communion with God and to increase our knowledge of God's word. It doesn't treat scripture as text simply to be studied, but as the living Word. It pays dividends to dwell on a passage in this way. Doing so with these verses in a group brought home to me how diverse we are. Each person conjured up their own image of what the scene might have been like that day, how it felt to be there in the throng. What visceral responses we each had to experiencing the scene from the inside, identifying variously with Mary, the onlookers or with Simeon himself gingerly taking the vulnerable child in his arms and beginning to burst forth with praise.

Nicola Slee has written a poem called 'Anna', which is surely the fruit of quietly meditating on this passage in the style of *lectio divina*. Just as she has done, let's imaginatively inhabit this story.

I've learnt how the Word comes
rising like fire from a thrown spark
or dropping like a stone
into the stilled mind's surface.
('Anna' by Nicola Slee)

DEBBIE THROWER

Transformation beckons

'Master, now you are dismissing your servant in peace, according to your word; for my eyes have seen your salvation, which you have prepared in the presence of all peoples, a light for revelation to the Gentiles and for glory to your people Israel.'

When places of worship closed on account of the pandemic, many were dismayed at no longer being allowed into church. The very bricks and mortar of sacred spaces hold a deep significance for us. Yet the coming of the Christ-child heralded a new era of worshipping 'in spirit and in truth'. We can now appreciate we live in a world where with every footfall we're treading on sacred ground. Just as the covenant and the law set apart the holy nation of Israel, so in Christ those promises are now for all who belong to him. We, too, are heirs of the treasures given to Abraham and Moses.

The temple was traditionally the place where God's presence was known. But as Jesus told the Samaritan woman at the well: 'The hour is coming, and is now here, when the true worshippers will worship the Father in spirit and truth, for the Father seeks such as these to worship him. God is spirit, and those who worship him must worship in spirit and truth' (John 4:23–24). Simeon stood in a long line of priestly men familiar with the sacrifices required to be in good stead with God. The cross has given access to grace for all peoples.

The story of Simeon and Anna, two such faithful people in their later years, emphasises the challenge of how we too might spend our life offering loving service to God and the world around us. What's true for them is true for us – once that truth is encountered, our life can never be the same again. Nothing less than transformation beckons.

Old as I am, and hollowed out by
prayer and silence and weeping and fasting,
I live for that quickening,
for the pouring that will rise up and overflow all containment,
that my own thirst may be kindled,
my body leap into flame.
('Anna' by Nicola Slee)

DEBBIE THROWER

Stabat mater

And the child's father and mother were amazed at what was being said about him. Then Simeon blessed them and said to his mother Mary, 'This child is destined for the falling and the rising of many in Israel, and to be a sign that will be opposed so that the inner thoughts of many will be revealed – and a sword will pierce your own soul too.'

I listened to the journalist Bel Mooney on the radio one day recalling the death of her stillborn baby son, Guy. The trauma, decades later, was still apparent in her voice. It was painful to hear. Her words evoked my own experience of miscarrying a baby many years ago, and the memory of the grief of that time came back forcefully.

'Stabat mater', the grieving mother of so much sacred art (of which Bel Mooney, incidentally, is a collector), is a haunting symbol of the sacrifices motherhood entails. Simeon's words are prophetic. Mary will be cut to the quick when she stands weeping beside the cross.

Mooney has redeemed her agonising experience of losing a son at birth, partly at least, by founding Sands, the stillbirth and neo-natal death charity (**sands.org.uk**). It was an article she wrote in the mid-1970s which paved the way for the charity and for countless bereaved couples to be helped. Nevertheless, there's much yet to be done to acknowledge the pain endured by parents in such circumstances.

The mother of Jesus would pay a high price for becoming the mother of God. The mother weeping her heart out is a potent image down through the ages. Mothers in so many different contexts today still shed tears for their offspring and, as was said in that same programme, a mother's, a parent's, role is to 'be strong' for their child.

Just to stand and wait may, indeed, be agony, but exercising restraint is, sometimes, all we are called to. 'They also serve who only stand and wait' is the final line of the poem 'On His Blindness' by John Milton.

Dear Lord, help us when we can do nothing more than wait for pain and grief to subside. Be with all who suffer and who mourn. Amen

DEBBIE THROWER

The presentation of Jesus

There was also a prophet, Anna the daughter of Phanuel, of the tribe of Asher.

Anna is a popular name, meaning gift or grace. It's an apt title, then, for Anna Chaplaincy for Older People – offering spiritual care as a gracious gift from a local church to its surrounding community. Anna Chaplains are there for people of any or no faith. It's about drawing alongside someone as a trusted companion.

While Simeon is widely believed to have been from the tribe of Levi, Anna was from the wrong side of the tracks, as it were. The tribe of Asher was not held in such high esteem. Luke wants us to realise it's no coincidence that Anna was in the temple, routinely at prayer, on that day of the Lord's presentation. Telling the story in this way shows the presentation as a moment of wholeness of the Jewish people, one in which the Messiah is received and recognised by both sides of the divide that had occurred centuries before.

The narrative of Simeon and Anna is a powerful narrative of both reconciliation and of hope. If I had to pick one word to sum up Anna Chaplaincy, it would be 'hope'.

It wasn't easy being an old woman, without relatives, at the time of Jesus, with no state aid. Such a lone woman past her working years would be impoverished and vulnerable. Anna had taken refuge in the temple and, possibly, lived off the scraps and whatever alms people gave her, should she even be noticed. I love the fact Jesus always seemed to spot people on the periphery. The story of the widow's two mites (Luke 21:1–4) echoes that of Anna.

I've learnt to live in silence,
every day offering my emptiness up
to mingle with the incense of the sacrifices burning on the altar.
I live on what the pilgrims give me
from the remains of their cooked meat,
when the priests have taken their fill.
('Anna' by Nicola Slee)

DEBBIE THROWER

Prophets of our time

She was of a great age, having lived with her husband for seven years after her marriage, then as a widow to the age of eighty-four. She never left the temple but worshipped there with fasting and prayer night and day. At that moment she came, and began to praise God and to speak about the child to all who were looking for the redemption of Jerusalem.

Anna is part of a tradition of women prophets: Miriam and Deborah in the Old Testament, for example, and Mary, the mother of Jesus, and other women who prophesy in the New Testament story of Pentecost (Acts 1:14; 2:17). I believe Anna Chaplains have a prophetic role today, speaking into a society which still marginalises women, particularly older women without much in the way of status or means.

It isn't easy growing old in the fast-changing 21st century. Anna Chaplains are navigators, helping men and women negotiate the choppy seas of growing old when age is not revered but feared, families often dispersed and fragmented. They're also interpreters, reading the signs of the times, pointing to new ways of regarding older age and encouraging us to see with the eyes of God.

I feel sure God doesn't think his children are 'over the hill' once they're over 40, or 'washed up', 'past their sell-by date' or in any way 'surplus to requirements', as older people are sometimes described so unkindly when they no longer conform to youthful standards of beauty or are no longer economically active. As John Bell of the Iona Community once said in a radio talk, 'God expects old dogs to do new tricks. God expects people whom the world would deem past it to initiate.'

The chief requirement of an Anna Chaplain – of whatever age, and many are women aged 60+ – is to be a good listener. Female or male, lay or ordained, Anna Chaplains hear the honest hopes, doubts and fears of people in a society that's rapidly ageing. We're in unprecedented territory when it comes to living longer: according to Age UK, the number of centenarians increased by 85% in the past 15 years.

Lord, help me grow old grace-fully. Help me remember I was created for change. Amen

DEBBIE THROWER

Psalms 71—84

I have three difficulties with the Psalms, but also some solutions to offer.

First, they are in no sort of order. We can, however, do a little rearranging to suit ourselves. For the next two weeks we will look at our psalms under three headings: we will begin with psalms about God – God as judge, as ruler and as victor – before moving on to psalms about the nation, and then end with a group of psalms on various other topics, some of them unusually interesting. So we will take them in subject order rather than in biblical sequence.

All of these psalms are prayers, except for 78 and 82, which are both teaching psalms. Psalm 78 is a potted but somewhat selective history of Israel from Moses to the building of Solomon's temple and is by far the longest psalm on our list.

Second, there are a number of psalms that ask God to slaughter my enemies. I can't think of anyone I would like God to deal with in that way at the moment. My prayer book sensibly leaves out these 'cursing verses', as they are known. In fact, it leaves out Psalm 83 – the worst offender in our group – entirely. Other psalms speak to situations I have simply never experienced.

There are many situations that confronted psalmists that we hope we will never have to face. When I was quite little, during World War II, my grandmother would get very fearful during air raids. I remember writing out some psalm verses for her and heading them 'Psalms for Air Raids'. Perhaps I should have chosen some cursing verses, such as Psalm 83:13–18. In wartime, we did have enemies, but who or what are our enemies now? The New Testament makes that pretty clear for us, as we shall see. Some of the psalms' cursing verses might be a good way to put the fear of God into our demonic enemies.

My third difficulty arises whenever a psalmist changes the subject in midstream. I am glad that happens only in one of the psalms we are going to be looking at – see the reflection on Psalm 71!

PAUL GRAVELLE

God the judge

'I have set a time for judgement,' says God, 'and I will judge with fairness. Though every living creature tremble and the earth itself be shaken, I will keep its foundations firm. I tell the wicked not to be arrogant; I tell them to stop their boasting.' Judgement does not come from the east or from the west, from the north or from the south; it is God who is the judge, condemning some and acquitting others.

When did you last hear a sermon about judgement? It is certainly not as popular a subject as it once was. Do we feel we don't need to hear about judgement any more because we are all forgiven anyway? Is it a subject that may be fine for street preachers but is no longer appropriate for church-goers who have already responded to God's call? However, the creeds still say things like 'He will come again in glory to judge the living and the dead', don't they?

Judgement for all is most certainly part of God's plan. I think many of you will, like me, always feel awfully uncomfortable when the last part of Matthew 25 is read in church. This is where Jesus describes the final judgement and the goats are separated from the sheep. I always think of the needy person in the street I failed to give to, or the sick person I failed to visit. There is never a shortage of failures like these.

There used to be a school of thought that said, 'Once saved, always saved,' a bit like the indulgences that monks used to peddle in the decadent days of the church before the Reformation and Counter-Reformation. No, Jesus would have endorsed what the psalmist says about there being a time set for judgement. The psalmist sounds a clear warning to the wicked, but, when he speaks of God judging with fairness, he adds that every living creature will tremble at the prospect.

There is, however, a word of comfort as well. Though the earth itself be shaken, says God, I will keep its foundations firm.

Thank you, Lord God, for your promise that our planet will endure until Jesus comes back to restore it.

PAUL GRAVELLE

God's justice

God is indeed good to Israel, to those who have pure hearts. But I had nearly lost confidence; my faith was almost gone because I was jealous of the proud when I saw that things go well for the wicked. They do not suffer pain; they are strong and healthy... Those who abandon you will certainly perish; you will destroy those who are unfaithful to you. But as for me, how wonderful to be near God, to find protection with the Sovereign Lord and to proclaim all that he has done!

The psalmist starts off pretty close to the mark here. Don't we all feel a bit like him at times? So many of the rich and famous allow their affluence to go to their heads, and it causes them to go off the rails. At least, that's the way we see it. It may not be universally true; it could be just the way the media is portraying it. But their wealth makes us envious, just like the psalmist.

If God is God, his justice must be perfect in every case. Yesterday we looked at God as judge; today we need to convince ourselves that God acts with perfect justice – he is unquestionably fair to all concerned and he is unswervingly unbiased in everything he does.

One of the ways to understand this a little better is to see God as a time traveller. God is eternal. He lives altogether outside of time. The Father and Jesus himself both laid claim to that mysterious name, I AM. Surely they mean by this that they are always in the present tense. In the eternal sphere, God *is* saving Israel by leading them though the Red Sea. Similarly, he *is* listening to the psalmist's prayer, as well as yours and mine. He *is* seated on his judgement throne, passing sentence on all whom the psalmist saw as abandoning him and committing every kind of subtle wickedness and atrocity. And he is doing these things all at the same instant!

Lord God, you say that you are I AM. We struggle to fully understand what that means. Help us to grasp what it means for us, as we live here in time. Amen

PAUL GRAVELLE

God the supreme ruler

God presides in the heavenly council; in the assembly of the gods he gives his decision: 'You must stop judging unjustly; you must no longer be partial to the wicked! Defend the rights of the poor and the orphans; be fair to the needy and the helpless. Rescue them from the power of evil people. How ignorant you are! How stupid! You are completely corrupt, and justice has disappeared from the world. "You are gods," I said; "all of you are children of the Most High." But you will die like mortals; your life will end like that of any prince.' Come, O God, and rule the world; all the nations are yours.

Here is an interesting psalm for us. It's sort of an Old Testament screenplay, starting with the stage setting and then giving God his lines to speak. But what is going on in this scene? Who are these lesser gods who are misbehaving themselves? What should we make of this rather curious, ancient dramatic fragment?

Some commentators seem to have a problem over solving this one. My take on it is simply this: there have always been rulers and leaders who think of themselves as demigods. We have had them in New Zealand, and no doubt you can name some wherever you live. And there will be evil people causing harm and injustice right down the line. You may be suffering from the effects of what they are doing right now. But our God is the only real God, the eternal one, the I AM.

Those who cause evil can only have been given their authority by God. They are still his children in the sense that he loves them and longs for them to return to sanity and to recognise him for who he truly is. The psalmist adds his plea to God at the end of the script: 'Come, O God, and rule the world.'

O Lord, we echo the psalmist's plea for so many of your true children in Asia, Africa and elsewhere who are suffering persecution, imprisonment and even death, reminding you, our God, of the angelic promise at the ascension – that Jesus will come back again.

PAUL GRAVELLE

God the victor

How glorious you are, O God! How majestic, as you return from the mountains where you defeated your foes… Give the Lord your God what you promised him; bring gifts to him, all you nearby nations. God makes everyone fear him; he humbles proud princes and terrifies great kings.

These verses remind me of the 'triumphs' accorded to victors in ancient Rome. Each Roman general longed for his 'triumph', when he could parade through the streets of Rome at the head of his legions, with a baggage train loaded with the spoils he had won and with defeated captives, soon to be sold as slaves. They would have been glorious but horrific spectacles!

The title of 'victor' is more usually given to Jesus, as in the Latin *Christus Victor*, and I particularly like to think of him in that way. When I left the air force in 1952, I did teacher training at St Mark and St John's College in Chelsea. At the entrance to the chancel in the wonderful Romanesque college chapel was an amazing 3D-sculptured plaque of *Christus Victor* – in red, purple and gilt, as I recall – showing Jesus as John describes him in the first chapter of Revelation and with his arms raised in victory. Sadly, I believe the plaque went missing when the college moved to Plymouth.

Jesus has won the greatest imaginable victory for us. He is the absolute victor over death itself, and everyone who recognises who Jesus is and that this victory is for them has already begun to live in eternal life.

I have a collection of crosses. Some I have bought in various countries, some I have been given and some I have made from different materials. I try to wear a different one every Sunday. Four of these crosses have a figure of Jesus Christ in glory – as we will all see him one wonderful day. *Christus Victor*!

If you get a chance to read Tom Wright's book Surprised by Hope, *you will find much there that relates to Christ's great victory and what it really means for us. But, as his title suggests, expect some surprises. Now I'm going to read it again!*

PAUL GRAVELLE

Longing for God's house

How I love your Temple, Lord Almighty! How I want to be there! I long to be in the Lord's Temple. With my whole being I sing for joy to the living God. Even the sparrows have built a nest, and the swallows have their own home; they keep their young near your altars, Lord Almighty, my king and my God. How happy are those who live in your Temple, always singing praises to you.

I write this as New Zealand is beginning to emerge from the Covid-19 pandemic. We have not been able to gather in church for the past eight Sundays, and this psalm is particularly real for us, just as it would have been for all of you – and maybe still is for some. We even have a sparrow that lives in or very near our church. We often only learn to value something when we find we can't have it.

Of course, it's not the building, it's the people who meet there, and God is present whenever his people meet. If we are prevented from going to church for a time, through illness, hospitalisation, work or whatever, we miss the people and the familiar form of service, and we especially miss Communion. But underneath these longings, what we are really missing is that special sense of God's presence that is there when God's people meet together.

The Jewish people were convinced that God lived in their temple. This is what the psalm is about, because when they were in exile they couldn't go to the temple. They were just like we were in lockdown.

How did we feel in those dark days? Here in New Zealand, where comparatively few died, a longing for God's house was perhaps a lesser concern than for those of you nearer to the crisis of 2020–21. How vital is it for you to be with God's people every Sunday, and would this psalm be your personal song if circumstances prevented you from being there?

Lord, it is so good when your people gather together in freedom and unity. Grant to all from whom that blessing is withheld that they may know again the freedom to worship you together.

PAUL GRAVELLE

A prayer for a king

Teach the king to judge with your righteousness, O God; share with him your own justice, so that he will rule over your people with justice and govern the oppressed with righteousness. May the land enjoy prosperity; may it experience righteousness. May the king judge the poor fairly; may he help the needy and defeat their oppressors. May your people worship you as long as the sun shines, as long as the moon gives light, for ages to come.

This is David's last psalm. It is most likely a prayer for his son Solomon, but it is thought by many to be also a prophetic poem about the coming Messiah. If this is so, we may want to read it in anticipation of the Messiah's second visit to Planet Earth, more so than with an eye to his first appearance as Jesus.

The psalm continues with prophetic statements regarding the king, some of which were fulfilled quite literally during Solomon's reign. Verses 10 and 15 prophesy that he will be given gold from Sheba, for example. The visit of the queen of that land fulfilled this. When, however, we read statements such as, 'All kings will bow down before him; all nations will serve him' (v. 11), we can only think of a Messiah who is yet to come.

We have the promise of the angels at Jesus' ascension – for angels are what those men in white must have been – that he will return. And this is indeed a messianic psalm, which looks forward not to the Jesus of the gospels – the Jesus we know – but to the Jesus of the future, having returned to earth in glory, who will fulfil every prophecy the scripture contains about him.

We have an amazing future ahead of us, for we will be there to see it all and to share God's renewed world. We were thinking about his role as judge earlier this week. Today we can look at the other side of this golden coin.

Lord Jesus, it is sometimes hard to believe that you really intend to come back and fulfil all the wonderful prophecies that are about you. Help us to keep our eyes on you, for you have promised never to leave us. Amen

PAUL GRAVELLE

A prayer for national deliverance (1)

Remember, O Lord, that your enemies laugh at you, that they are godless and despise you. Don't abandon your helpless people to their cruel enemies; don't forget your persecuted people! Remember the covenant you made with us. There is violence in every dark corner of the land. Don't let the oppressed be put to shame; let those poor and needy people praise you. Rouse yourself, God, and defend your cause! Remember that godless people laugh at you all day long. Don't forget the angry shouts of your enemies, the continuous noise made by your foes.

In the earlier verses of this psalm, this psalmist is bemoaning the destruction of the temple by Israel's enemies. Now he is getting down to reminding God of his responsibilities towards his people. And he gets quite heated about it! Have you ever told God to 'rouse himself'? Maybe not, but there will most likely have been times when each of us wanted to say something like that when it seemed as if God was not hearing us or, if he was, not answering in the way we would like.

The psalmist never got the answer he wanted. The real opportunity for deliverance came when a carpenter from Nazareth began to teach and work miracles among the people. But, as we know, the people failed to recognise this as the deliverance God was offering. God often works like that. He answers our prayers in ways that we fail to recognise. But there is one thing of particular interest in this psalm: although it begins by reminding God that his temple has been ruined, the main petition is not for the restoration of the structure but the deliverance of God's people.

So, if you are feeling overwhelmed by the evil you see and hear around you, this part of the psalm could be a good prayer for you. Remember, however, that God is not unaware of it and is working things out for the ultimate good of us all, as we shall see one day!

Thank you, Lord, that you work in mysterious ways, your wonders to perform. Please make sure that we recognise what you are doing and give you the thanks and praise you deserve. Amen

PAUL GRAVELLE

A prayer for national deliverance (2)

Lord, will you be angry with us forever? Will your anger continue to burn like fire? Turn your anger on the nations that do not worship you, on the people who do not pray to you. For they have killed your people; they have ruined your country. Do not punish us for the sins of our ancestors. Have mercy on us now; we have lost all hope. Help us, O God, and save us; rescue us and forgive our sins for the sake of your own honour... Listen to the groans of the prisoners, and by your great power free those who are condemned to die.

It is good to pray for our nation. For some, myself included, that will mean praying for more than one nation – that of our birth and the one where we now live, for example. For the Jewish people in Old Testament times, it was the custom to pray for punishment to be meted out to the enemies who were causing the present anguish. In this psalm, however, we find some recognition that they had brought the present calamities on themselves: 'Do not punish us for the sins of our ancestors... rescue us and forgive our sins for the sake of your own honour.' The psalmist at least acknowledges that Israel's own sins, past and present, have brought down God's anger upon them.

There is a move afoot here in New Zealand that Christians have a responsibility to repent on behalf of the nation for the wrongdoing that they can see is affecting its moral health and well-being. Have we, as Christians, really presented a united front against the evils of substance abuse in our respective countries, for example?

The final verse in today's passage stood out for me because I hear so much about our brother and sister Christians who, in a number of countries, are held in prison simply on account of their faith in Jesus Christ.

I am sorry if you feel I have added to your prayer load. There are so many worthy causes that are calling for and deserving of our prayers in these troubled days. Just pray for those which touch your heart.

PAUL GRAVELLE

A prayer for national restoration

Bring us back, Almighty God! Show us your mercy, and we will be saved! You brought a grapevine out of Egypt; you drove out other nations and planted it in their land… Why did you break down the fences around it? Now anyone passing by can steal its grapes; wild hogs trample it down, and wild animals feed on it. Turn to us, Almighty God! Look down from heaven at us; come and save your people! Come and save this grapevine that you planted, this young vine you made grow so strong!

This psalmist has got it all wrong. He is encouraging the people – for this is a liturgical psalm for use in public worship – to pray that everything will be put back as it was before. Look at the phrases he uses: 'Bring us back'; 'Why did you break down the fences around it?'; 'Save this grapevine which you planted.'

God's promise to Abraham was that all nations would be blessed through his descendants, but the Jewish people had forgotten about this and thought that God's blessing was just for them. The grapevine idea is beautiful, but how much better if the psalm could use new thoughts like: 'Take us forward, extend this grapevine so that all nations may gather its fruit!'

Do you sometimes suffer from nostalgia? I do. I look back to the 1960s and 1970s when the Holy Spirit seemed to have fallen on God's people afresh and we saw and heard of wonderful manifestations of God's power almost daily, so it seemed. But we are living in today's world. Whatever the circumstances may be, we are still God's people, called, just as the Jewish people were, to bless people of every nation with the good news of Jesus and his promise of eternal life.

We have everything to look forward to. Let's not spend time wishing for the 'good old days' of full churches; rather let's pray for daily opportunities to bless people of all nations with the good news that we now know.

Lord, please give me at least one opportunity today to be a blessing to someone who has never yet experienced the love of Jesus.

PAUL GRAVELLE

A song for a festival

Shout for joy to God our defender; sing praise to the God of Jacob! Start the music and beat the tambourines; play pleasant music on the harps and the lyres. Blow the trumpet for the festival, when the moon is new and when the moon is full. This is the law in Israel, an order from the God of Jacob. He gave it to the people of Israel when he attacked the land of Egypt… 'But my people would not listen to me; Israel would not obey me.'

All this sounds pretty familiar, doesn't it? The world has just celebrated Christmas, but how many really understood what the celebration was commemorating? Unless Jesus returns before then, it will be just the same at Easter.

We think these thoughts at festival times every year. Why don't people come to church, at least at Christmas and Easter, the way they used to? There will be a number of answers to this question. Some could be traced to inadequacies in the social or education systems; others may centre around the awareness of the local church to the needs of the people in its locality. When it comes down to it, however, one basic solution to the problem is for you and me to be ready to say to the people next door – and better still, up and down our street – 'Will you come to church with me this Christmas?' and 'You'll come to church with us for Easter, won't you?'

This sounds as if I'm thinking only about great festival celebrations. Every Sunday is a celebration for God's people. I will never forget a brave man telling me that the scariest thing he had ever done was to come through the door of his local church on his own for the very first time on an ordinary Sunday morning.

The biggest reason of all why people do not come these days may be because they do not know what to expect and they are scared.

Dear Lord, I am so scared to ask other people to come to church with me.
Help me to remember that they are even more scared to come on their own
without me. Amen

PAUL GRAVELLE

Comfort in distress

I cry aloud to God; I cry aloud, and he hears me. In times of trouble I pray to the Lord; all night long I lift my hands in prayer, but I cannot find comfort. When I think of God, I sigh; when I meditate, I feel discouraged. He keeps me awake all night; I am so worried that I cannot speak. I think of days gone by and remember years of long ago... Everything you do, O God, is holy. No god is as great as you. You are the God who works miracles; you showed your might among the nations.

I cannot imagine anyone who cannot empathise with the psalmist here. Every one of us has experienced days and nights like those described here, when everything in our world collapses and God is somewhere else – or so it seems. We have lost a loved one or our home, we have been made redundant or we have been diagnosed with a terminal illness. Any of these things, and indeed many others, can put us in the same state of distress in which the psalmist finds himself.

It is always so hard to discern where God is when we find ourselves in situations like this. The psalmist acknowledges that God is all-powerful, but can you sympathise with his unspoken cry, 'Where are you, God! What are you going to do to help me now?' Often, when we are in troubled circumstances like this, God sends someone along to share our burden of sorrow – usually someone who has been through the same trouble themselves. This is his way of bringing the comfort we need.

But maybe things are going well for you at the moment. Or at least things are not quite as bad for you as they are for some others. If that is so, it may be that God is nudging you right now and saying, 'I wonder if you could go along and hold ___'s hand. They're in need of a little bit of comfort.'

Lord, is there some situation where you want me to offer comfort and support? I feel so inadequate. But, if you come with me, I will. Where do you want us to go – together?

PAUL GRAVELLE

A history lesson

Listen, my people, to my teaching, and pay attention to what I say. I am going to use wise sayings and explain mysteries from the past, things we have heard and known, things that our ancestors told us. We will not keep them from our children; we will tell the next generation about the Lord's power and his great deeds and the wonderful things he has done... In this way they also will put their trust in God and not forget what he has done, but always obey his commandments.

This psalm is a history lesson for young Israelites, teaching them a good slice of their nation's past. I made an exciting discovery recently. Historians have traditionally judged the authenticity of ancient documents by applying four criteria: quality, quantity of copies, early date and authorship. A more advanced system has now been developed using eight further criteria, such as eyewitness accounts and independent attestation. When all these twelve criteria are applied to the four gospels, the facts about Jesus are considered by historians to be unimpeachable. The words and actions of Jesus are far better authenticated than those of other figures of the period, such as Hannibal or Nero.

Do you know someone who attempts to discredit Christianity on scientific grounds? There are one or two in my family. We can now talk to them from an historical perspective, just like the psalmist. Everything that Jesus said and did is now authenticated 'beyond reasonable doubt'. We might say that, even though the existence of God can't be proved scientifically, what God has done on earth as Jesus Christ has now been unequivocally proven. It is legally true!

So, where do we go from here? Well, I feel a new confidence. I can look anyone in the eye with a new assurance. But also, and more importantly, I can now turn my faith in a new direction, believing that, as a Christian, I have the miraculous power which Jesus says is given to all believers.

Lord Jesus, help us to believe what you have said – that believers will be given the power to perform miracles. May we see that power manifest. Amen

PAUL GRAVELLE

Defeat of God's enemies

O God, do not keep silent; do not be still, do not be quiet! Look! Your enemies are in revolt, and those who hate you are rebelling. They are making secret plans against your people; they are plotting against those you protect… Cover their faces with shame, O Lord, and make them acknowledge your power. May they be defeated and terrified forever; may they die in complete disgrace. May they know that you alone are the Lord, supreme ruler over all the earth.

No wonder they leave this one out when psalms are sung. We're taught to love our enemies, not to curse them, aren't we? Yes, but what about our spiritual enemies? 'Resist the Devil, and he will run away from you' (James 4:7), and James is not alone in giving that advice. Look at the way Jesus dealt with all who came to him under the control of evil spirits.

Christians of the first century knew how to deal with the servant spirits of Satan. They told them to go back to where they belong. They did it fearlessly in the name of Jesus, and the demon spirits obeyed, knowing that they were powerless against the name of Jesus.

Spiritual warfare is not just about dealing with temptation. Writing to the Ephesians about putting on the whole armour of God, Paul says that we are not fighting against human enemies, but against 'the wicked spiritual forces in the heavenly world, the rulers, authorities and cosmic powers of this dark age' (Ephesians 6:12).

Jesus told Peter that the gates of hell would not be able to stand against the church. We are sometimes tempted to think that those 'gates' are somehow on the move against us. But the reverse is true: gates are defence mechanisms, and we are on the attack. Believe it! Let's use the spiritual gift of discernment to recognise whatever the enemy is up to.

Lord God, release in us the gift of spiritual discernment, that we may recognise every trick of our enemy Satan, both in this world and in our lives, and by your power within us resist him and cause him to flee from us. Amen

PAUL GRAVELLE

An old person's prayer

Lord, I have come to you for protection; never let me be defeated!... I have relied on you all my life; you have protected me since the day I was born. I will always praise you... I will tell of your goodness; all day long I will speak of your salvation, though it is more than I can understand... Now that I am old and my hair is grey, do not abandon me, O God! Be with me while I proclaim your power and might to all generations to come.

When I was six, my mother woke me up to look at a bright glow in the sky. The Crystal Palace was on fire! So perhaps I am old enough to use this psalm.

This is a poem of lament by an old man who starts off feeling abandoned by God. Hebrew laments traditionally follow a pattern of appeal, complaint, petition and thanksgiving, but our aged psalmist breaks all the rules. He starts with an appeal, then switches to reminiscence, and then from abject bargaining with God to outright flattery. We get like that when we are old; we have a shorter attention span at times, I suppose.

Do we sometimes slip into the old psalmist's trap of trying to bargain with God? You know what I mean: 'God, if you do this for me, I promise to invite so-and-so to the next Alpha course.' I am sure that God must have loved that old psalmist very dearly. He loves you and me in just the same way. He doesn't need our flattery. He certainly doesn't want us to try to bargain with him. But he really treasures our worship – when we express our love and praises back to him personally, rather than just saying or singing things like that *about* him to others. And, of course, he does love to hear our petitions too.

Lord, help me to shape my prayers to the pattern Jesus taught, because you are so holy. We need your kingdom here on earth. Meet my needs and forgive my failures because you are the king of time and all eternity. Amen

PAUL GRAVELLE

Ecclesiastes:
enjoying life with God in the real world

The opening words of the Teacher in the book of Ecclesiastes are 'Meaningless! Meaningless!... Utterly meaningless! Everything is meaningless!' (1:2, NIV), giving us the first impression that it is going to be a pessimistic and depressing read. Far from it! Yes, Ecclesiastes is a huge reality check, but there is optimism and hope – life is far from pointless.

The author, whom some consider to be Solomon and others a later writer, has been on a lifelong quest to discover the nature of wisdom and how humans can find meaning and enjoyment in life. He shares his findings with the faith assembly using persuasive public-speaking techniques: repetition, rhetorical questions, hyperbole, emotive narratives and images, powerful language, anecdotes, observations, sayings, riddles, reflection, advice, instruction and, finally, strong conclusions. He is a preacher as well as a teacher. Sometimes his opinions can appear to contradict, leaving us to work out when one piece of advice should be followed and when another.

Ecclesiastes is certainly a book to grapple with, but it is well worth the effort, for it has insights that enable us to grow in Christian wisdom and maturity, which we discover is less about study and knowledge and more about enjoying life with God in the real world.

The Teacher leads us to consider three strands. First, we will contemplate our relationship with God. Second, we will reflect on recognising, acknowledging and accepting the human 'lot' (one of the Teacher's expressions). We will find in that knowledge, instead of despair, both relief and freedom, for we are given permission to drop the pretence that human life is any other than how we experience it, with its repetitiveness, complexities and sorrows. In so doing, we gain a wisdom that empowers us to put into practice the third strand: balanced living that brings enjoyment. These three strands, when intertwined, produce a cord that cannot easily be broken, giving us strength and resilience.

FIONA STRATTA

The Teacher's conclusion

Vanity of vanities, says the Teacher; all is vanity. Besides being wise, the Teacher also taught the people knowledge, weighing and studying and arranging many proverbs. The Teacher sought to find pleasing words, and he wrote words of truth plainly. The sayings of the wise are like goads, and like nails firmly fixed are the collected sayings that are given by one shepherd... The end of the matter; all has been heard. Fear God, and keep his commandments; for that is the whole duty of everyone.

In the introduction I described the Teacher's life journey as a quest. It could also be seen as a scientific experiment, in which he investigates life. These verses are the final conclusion of his experiment: 'Vanity of vanities; all is vanity,' the Teacher relentlessly pronounces.

The word 'vanity' is a translation of the Hebrew word *hevel*, meaning a breath or vapour. William Thackeray describes *Vanity Fair* as a 'world where everyone is striving for what is not worth having' (*Vanity Fair*, 1848). Like Thackeray, the Teacher does not hide from this bleak reality but writes the 'truth plainly'. All in this life is transient. Plans may not be fulfilled and promises may end up being empty. Our experiences in life, in matters of politics, work, achievement, relationships, leisure or pleasure, can at times seem random and meaningless.

This makes for uncomfortable reading. Indeed, the Teacher's words *should* be uncomfortable for us at times, just as a sheep finds the shepherd's goad (a spiked stick) unpleasant. The shepherd does, however, sometimes need to give the sheep a firm but loving prod to stop it from straying. The sayings and wisdom of Ecclesiastes can act as goads, spurring us on in the right direction. The 'nails firmly fixed' are needed to make a construction stable. Likewise the Teacher's words have the potential to bring us stability, security, peace and joy. Trusting in the Lord's gentle discipline, we sometimes need to feel the discomfort of the goad or the pain of the nails being hammered home before we can be healed.

Lord, thank you that wisdom begins with fearing you. May we keep your commandments central in our lives, loving you with all our heart, soul, strength and mind and loving our neighbours as we love ourselves.

FIONA STRATTA

Remember your creator

A person can do nothing better than to eat and drink and find satisfaction in their own toil. This too, I see, is from the hand of God, for without him, who can eat or find enjoyment? To the person who pleases him, God gives wisdom, knowledge and happiness… Guard your steps when you go to the house of God. Go near to listen… Do not be quick with your mouth, do not be hasty in your heart to utter anything before God. God is in heaven and you are on earth, so let your words be few.

Another of the Teacher's conclusions is that we should 'remember' our creator (12:1) from our youth onwards. How do we do this? In the above verses, the Teacher tells us he has realised that everything is a gift from God. We remember our creator when we acknowledge God's gifts with gratitude, especially the simple and routine everyday activities that can so easily be taken for granted, such as eating and drinking. Even the ability to enjoy our work and leisure comes as a gift from God, who wishes us to experience peace, satisfaction and joy as we journey through life. To do this we need the wisdom to live astutely, thereby making life-enhancing decisions.

Recalling the Lord's goodness is central to remembering our creator, as is taking time to worship him. We are instructed to approach worship with the right frame of mind. 'The house of God' refers to the temple. As the people drew near, its stunning appearance would have spoken to them of God's power, majesty and beauty, his 'otherness'. We, too, can be drawn to worship, not only by creation but also when we admire the splendour of churches, abbeys and cathedrals. Our recognition that 'God is in heaven' and we are 'on earth' reminds us that we should come to God humbly and ready to receive, not puffed up with what we consider we have to offer him. 'Going near to listen' speaks of our need for silence, meditation and contemplation. We are to enjoy the giver's gifts, but we are to focus on the giver.

We praise you, Lord, that you are our creator. Yours is the greatness, the splendour, the power, the glory and the majesty.

FIONA STRATTA

Acknowledging our limitations and the mystery

He has put a sense of past and future into their minds, yet they cannot find out what God has done from the beginning to the end… I know that whatever God does endures forever; nothing can be added to it, nor anything taken from it; God has done this, so that all should stand in awe before him… Consider the work of God; who can make straight what he has made crooked?… I said, 'I will be wise', but it was far from me… Just as you do not know how the breath comes to the bones in the mother's womb, so you do not know the work of God, who makes everything… Indeed, they do not know what is to be, for who can tell them how it will be?

God has given us enquiring minds: a thirst for knowledge and a desire to search out answers. We want to understand how our bodies and minds work, reflect on history and the universe – we have 'a sense of past and future'. The NIV translates this phrase as God having 'set eternity in the human heart', suggesting that God also placed within us a yearning for spiritual understanding.

Nonetheless, the Teacher tells us that our knowledge, ability and wisdom will always be limited. We don't even have the capacity to straighten a crooked stick! In God's wisdom, we cannot see what is around the corner. However much we study and whatever our reasoning powers, we will never have all the answers. The Teacher had a freedom-giving breakthrough when he realised that he could never attain the wisdom he was seeking. 'It was far from me', does not sound like a cry of despair, but of discernment. Discovering that he could not make himself wise was, in fact, a very wise moment!

Knowing our limitations and accepting them sets us free to appreciate the mystery of life, and to experience joy as we marvel at all God has made. This does not mean that we should give up on our pursuit of wisdom; rather, we should seek it as a gift from God through the Holy Spirit.

Lord, may we live with humility and a sense of the mystery of life, filled with awe, wonder and curiosity.

FIONA STRATTA

Acknowledging the ebb and flow

There is a time for everything, and a season for every activity under the heavens: a time to be born and a time to die, a time to plant and a time to uproot, a time to kill and a time to heal, a time to tear down and a time to build, a time to weep and a time to laugh, a time to mourn and a time to dance... Do not say, 'Why were the old days better than these?' For it is not wise to ask such questions... When times are good, be happy; but when times are bad, consider this: God has made the one as well as the other.

We come now to the best-known verses in Ecclesiastes and to another stark truth: there will be ebbs and flows in life that we are powerless to change. If we accept that ebbs will come, we will be less devastated by the blows, frustrations and disappointments that they bring. A deep trust in God's sovereignty will help us as we move through happy and sad times. While we can expect changes of seasons in our lives, we do not have to live in dread of them. With the help of the Holy Spirit we can not only survive the tough times, but thrive through them. We can be 'sorrowful' yet 'rejoicing' (2 Corinthians 6:10). It is as if we are living in two seasons simultaneously, experiencing both the 'best of times' and the 'worst of times', 'the spring of hope' and 'the winter of despair', as Charles Dickens wrote at the start of *A Tale of Two Cities* (1859).

During the ebbs, we are wise to avoid nostalgic musings, questioning life's turns and wishing we were back in seemingly better days. Such recollections increase our anguish and open the door to bitterness, wasting the present opportunities. There is a freedom to be found in acknowledging our vulnerability and in accepting that much of life is beyond our control. We trust in God's care and wait in hope for the returning 'flow'.

Lord, in the ebbs of life, help us to trust that 'all things work together for good for those who love God, who are called according to his purpose' (Romans 8:28, NRSV).

FIONA STRATTA

Acknowledging the uncertainties

Send out your bread upon the waters, for after many days you will get it back. Divide your means seven ways, or even eight, for you do not know what disaster may happen on earth… In the morning sow your seed, and at evening do not let your hands be idle; for you do not know which will prosper, this or that, or whether both alike will be good… Whatever your hand finds to do, do with your might.

Ambitious maritime trade was rapidly developing at the time that Ecclesiastes was written, so the expression 'Send out your bread upon the waters' is likely to be referring to making investments in seafaring commerce. However, life is uncertain, and we do not know for sure that what we invest in (financially, relationally or with time and effort) will succeed. So, to use a more modern expression, it is wise not to put all our eggs into one basket.

Fear of uncertainty or failure can paralyse us, stopping us from making decisions or taking action. The Teacher warns us not to fall into this trap, but to 'go for it', throwing ourselves into our activities. Although we will aim to make decisions carefully, living life fully will inevitably involve some risk. Once we have inwardly acknowledged that uncertainty cannot be eliminated, we are then free to take opportunities and engage in life, maximising our influence for good. We are free to start exploring ventures, even as some have to be discontinued because they have not worked out as planned. Who knows what can be achieved when we aim high for God? Who knows what will come from small beginnings?

An inner freedom comes as we let go of the desire to make life predictable and perfect. Whatever our age, we can dream dreams and have visions. We can choose to build up treasure in heaven. We can decide to be involved with people in prayer and in action. We can support projects that are bringing God's kingdom on earth.

'But seek first his kingdom and his righteousness, and all these things will be given to you as well. Therefore do not worry about tomorrow, for tomorrow will worry about itself. Each day has enough trouble of its own'
(Matthew 6:33–34, NIV).

FIONA STRATTA

Acknowledging the injustice

Again I looked and saw all the oppression that was taking place under the sun: I saw the tears of the oppressed – and they have no comforter; power was on the side of their oppressors… If you see the poor oppressed in a district, and justice and rights denied, do not be surprised at such things… I have seen something else under the sun: The race is not to the swift or the battle to the strong, nor does food come to the wise or wealth to the brilliant or favour to the learned; but time and chance happen to them all.

The Teacher instructs us not to be shocked at the evil of injustice. His realistic observation is that life is inherently unfair. We can see this in the world of politics and economics in more recent history and today – corrupt ideology and leaders destroy nations. The powerful can seem to get away with bad behaviour at best and atrocities at worst. Human rights abuse is as rampant now as it was then. It can be seen in the widespread persecution of minority groups and the cruelties of modern slavery. In the knowledge of this, we can either react with passive cynicism or choose to fight injustice and to meet the needs of others with compassion in whatever ways are possible.

However, the Teacher does not just refer to systemic injustices; he also talks about the unfairness that individuals face. Although sin usually implodes, and the godly usually reap the harvest for the good sown, this is not always the case. Usually but not always: it is this randomness that is hard to accept, this ambiguity that we struggle with, particularly when it affects those we love. Talent may be overlooked, while lesser aptitude receives acclaim; hard work may not be recognised and rewarded; academic success may not open up opportunities in life. We seek God's strength and grace to meet such challenges and to prevent resentment or pessimism from taking root.

Lord, save us from bitterness and despair when we are treated unfairly. May we never contribute, even unwittingly, to injustice, by being a fly in the ointment that gives off a bad odour (10:1), but instead be part of the solution, bringing the fragrance of Christ.

FIONA STRATTA

45

Acknowledging human nature, sin and judgement

And I saw something else under the sun: in the place of judgement – wickedness was there, in the place of justice – wickedness was there. I said to myself, 'God will bring into judgement both the righteous and the wicked, for there will be a time for every activity, a time to judge every deed'... Indeed, there is no one on earth who is righteous, no one who does what is right and never sins... This only have I found: God created mankind upright, but they have gone in search of many schemes... One sinner destroys much good.

As we have seen, the ebbs and flows, injustices and uncertainties can result in life feeling random and chaotic – 'meaningless'. In these verses, the Teacher goes to the core of the problem: although God has made everything good, 'beautiful in its time' (3:11), all humans harm themselves, others and the world through sin. We are not to be naive, for sin is very destructive – one action or bad choice can cause much damage. Life 'under the sun' is messy. In such a world, we should not 'chase the wind', expecting from life a perfection that it cannot offer.

For those who have been wronged or oppressed in this life, there is great solace in knowing that God is both comforter and judge: ultimately all will be well. For us all, there is the challenge to live wisely when we consider future judgement. Nevertheless, we can know peace of mind and freedom from the fear of condemnation, for we live in the light of what the Teacher did not foresee – God sent his son, Jesus Christ, to live a sinless life, in whose death and resurrection we receive forgiveness. Part of our discipleship involves living in ongoing repentance as we become conscious of ways in which we need to become more Christlike. A form of the 16th-century prayer of examen is a helpful practice at the end of each day: expressing gratitude for the day's gifts; reflecting on awareness of God's presence during the day; and confessing thoughts, words and deeds that have quenched the Spirit.

'If we confess our sins, he is faithful and just and will forgive us our sins and purify us from all unrighteousness' (1 John 1:9).

FIONA STRATTA

Acknowledging the inevitable

It is better to go to a house of mourning than to go to a house of feasting, for death is the destiny of everyone; the living should take this to heart... The heart of the wise is in the house of mourning, but the heart of fools is in the house of pleasure... Remember him – before the silver cord is severed, and the golden bowl is broken... and the dust returns to the ground it came from, and the spirit returns to God who gave it.

On superficial reading, we could find an apparent contradiction here. The Teacher has previously recommended enjoying life, including eating and drinking ('a house of feasting'), but now he states that it is better to go to 'a house of mourning'. What he is actually advising is that we come to terms with our own mortality, rather than hiding from it by means of endless distractions. Mourning with those who mourn, advocated in the above verses, is a sobering experience, but one that increases our grasp of the fleeting nature of life and therefore the wise use of our time on earth.

Dying is not an easy subject to discuss, hence why there are so many euphemisms for death, such as 'passed away', 'departed', 'gone home' and even 'underneath the daisies'. Compared to previous generations, we have been protected from the close proximity of death by modern standards of hygiene and medical advances. However, Covid-19 has reminded us of the fragility of life, bringing the 'D word' to the forefront of our thoughts once again. The Teacher had no qualms in speaking about death, suggesting that the way to freedom from the fear of death is through accepting our certain destiny and then getting on with living. He is promoting neither a morbid focus on death nor a desperate attitude of 'eat, drink, for tomorrow we die'.

Living after the coming of Christ, we have a steadfast hope of eternal life rooted in his resurrection. Like the apostle Paul, we can say, 'To me, to live is Christ and to die is gain' (Philippians 1:21).

'I shall be safely sheltered with the One who loves me best —
For underneath the daisies means to be at home with God'
('Underneath the Daisies' by Agnes Neale, 1890).

FIONA STRATTA

A balanced seeking after knowledge and wisdom

I said to myself… 'I have experienced much of wisdom and knowledge.' Then I applied myself to the understanding of wisdom, and also of madness and folly, but I learned that this, too, is a chasing after the wind. For with much wisdom comes much sorrow; the more knowledge, the more grief… Do not be over-righteous, neither be overwise – why destroy yourself?… Of making many books there is no end, and much study wearies the body… They seldom reflect on the days of their life, because God keeps them occupied with gladness of heart… A person's wisdom brightens their face and changes its hard appearance.

We have looked at the harsh realities of life through the Teacher's eyes and, in the light of this, now turn to the question, 'How then should we live?' The Teacher tells us that life is all about fearing God and avoiding extremes (7:18). We need to seek balance in all aspects of life.

The Teacher has advocated wisdom as being beneficial, and yet here he tells us not to be 'overwise'. Why? Too much reflection on what is happening in the world can rob us of joy. This does not mean turning a blind eye, but at times we may need to limit the amount of news we consume for the sake of our well-being. Likewise, although self-examination has its place in the Christian life, too much introspection is unhelpful, even destructive. We need to remain outward-looking and healthily occupied.

We are to avoid being 'over-righteous'. When through study we have developed a high level of knowledge, a pitfall is to become proud and self-righteous. Studying is enriching, but in realising how much there is still to learn, we must avoid overworking and burnout. Knowing when to stop is a wise principle that goes beyond studying. We also need to be shrewd, for we live in an age when information is plentiful and easily accessed but is not necessarily accurate.

Lord, help us to live with balance, wisdom and humility,
in a way that maximises our well-being and brings you glory.
Thank you that you are the source and giver of wisdom.

FIONA STRATTA

A balanced attitude towards pleasure and achievements

I said to myself, 'Come now, I will test you with pleasure to find out what is good.' But that also proved to be meaningless. 'Laughter,' I said, 'is madness. And what does pleasure accomplish?'… I undertook great projects: I built houses for myself and planted vineyards. I made gardens and parks and planted all kinds of fruit trees in them… I denied myself nothing my eyes desired; I refused my heart no pleasure. My heart took delight in all my labour, and this was the reward for all my toil. Yet… everything was meaningless, a chasing after the wind.

The Teacher has gained pleasure and fulfilment from the execution of his projects. We most likely can identify with this, albeit on a much smaller scale. God's gifts are for us to enjoy, so taking pleasure in our projects and ventures is not wrong or self-indulgent. Our ability to be creative is part of what it means to be made in the image of our creator. However, it is important to enjoy the process of our creative activity (the journey) because the end result (the destination), even if pleasing, can feel like an anti-climax.

The Teacher discovered through his search for contentment the law of diminishing returns – the more he put into pleasure-seeking, the less satisfaction he received in return. Ultimately, he was not fulfilled by his activities. God has not designed us to find inner meaning in pleasure and achievement. Many who have achieved the fame and fortune they have sought, enabling them to lead a life of leisure and pleasure, find only emptiness.

God has placed within humans a thirst that finds satisfaction from being loved by and loving their creator. As Christians, we know that Jesus promised to satisfy our spiritual thirst with living water through the Holy Spirit. We have the freedom to go against the flow in an achievement-motivated and pleasure-seeking society. We do this by committing ourselves, without being driven, to all God has given us to do and by regarding pleasure as a blessing rather than as a right.

Lord, may we find our greatest joy by placing our hope in you, 'who richly provides us with everything for our enjoyment' (1 Timothy 6:17, NRSV).

FIONA STRATTA

A balanced attitude towards possessions

Whoever loves money never has enough; whoever loves wealth is never satisfied with their income. This too is meaningless. As goods increase, so do those who consume them. And what benefit are they to the owners except to feast their eyes on them?… Moreover, when God gives someone wealth and possessions, and the ability to enjoy them, to accept their lot and be happy in their toil – this is a gift of God… A feast is made for laughter, wine makes life merry, and money is the answer for everything.

We can fall into a trap, the Teacher tells us, by thinking that life would be fundamentally different if only we had more money or certain possessions. Today we see only too plainly that consumerism feeds greed and vice versa, resulting in restless striving. Beautiful homes, clothes and possessions may be lovely to look at, but they do not feed our souls. In this way they are meaningless, empty, 'vanities'.

Receiving and enjoying all we have as a gift from God brings with it a different approach to our possessions. It is all about stewardship rather than ownership. We are called to share our possessions (for example, through hospitality), blessing others and being blessed in return. Rather than seeking more, we discover that contentment is wanting what we have, not having what we want! We enjoy God in everything and enjoy everything in God.

The Teacher does not want us to be naive about money, and he is certainly not suggesting that we should not fight poverty, for, he says, 'money is the answer for everything'. We do have to think about jobs, pay, pensions and savings, for this is God's usual way of providing for us to enjoy our lives. Balance is again the key: we are to be neither greedy nor ascetic in our approach to possessions. In contemporary society we have a responsibility to consider the sourcing of our possessions, making it our priority to buy ethically. Caring for the planet through thoughtful purchasing, as well as ensuring that the people who have made the goods we wish to buy have been treated fairly, are important considerations. Our enjoyment should not be at the expense of others.

'But godliness with contentment is great gain' (1 Timothy 6:6).

FIONA STRATTA

A balanced attitude towards work

For a person may labour with wisdom, knowledge and skill, and then they must leave all they own to another who has not toiled for it… What do people get for all the toil and anxious striving with which they labour under the sun? All their days their work is grief and pain; even at night their minds do not rest. This too is meaningless… So I saw that there is nothing better for a person than to enjoy their work, because that is their lot… So I commend the enjoyment of life… eat and drink and be glad. Then joy will accompany them in their toil.

Work, whether paid or unpaid, is another area in which the Teacher wants us to find balance. We are to avoid both laziness (4:5), which leads to self-destruction and ruin, and 'anxious striving', which results in stress, an inability to relax and poor sleep patterns. The Teacher has studied compulsive workaholics and can see that the lifestyle is harmful. Work–life balance is a hot topic in the 21st century, and we would do well to heed the Teacher's conclusion: 'Better one handful with tranquillity than two handfuls with toil and chasing after the wind' (4:6). We need to make time to enjoy leisure and relaxation, for this re-energises us to work effectively.

Our work is an important part of our 'lot' in life that can bring both satisfaction and enjoyment. For many people, work is closely linked to a sense of identity and purpose. Retirement can therefore be a hard adaption. The arrival of Covid-19 changed working life dramatically. A shift to working from home, already on the increase, accelerated rapidly. For some this was positive, giving flexibility and freeing up previously lost time spent commuting. For others, working from home increased the stress of their working lives, as they missed the camaraderie of the work environment and even a quiet place in which to work. Many lost work and others are fearful of the new uncertainties affecting the workplace. As Christians, we can prayerfully and practically support those who are struggling.

Lord, may we work for you with enthusiasm and encourage others, always remembering that our true identity and purpose are in Christ, rather than in our work.

FIONA STRATTA

Balanced relationships

Two are better than one, because they have a good return for their labour: if either of them falls down, one can help the other up. But pity anyone who falls and has no one to help them up... A cord of three strands is not quickly broken... Patience is better than pride. Do not be quickly provoked in your spirit, for anger resides in the lap of fools... Calmness can lay great offences to rest... Words from the mouth of the wise are gracious, but fools are consumed by their own lips.

One of the problems with striving for wealth and possessions or having a poor work–life balance is that relationships suffer. Ecclesiastes is peppered with advice on creating and preserving good relationships. Although the Teacher's well-known words are often applied to marriage, they are also relevant to friendship and team-working. Healthy relationships are respectful, mutually supportive and enable flourishing. Relationships are damaged by pride, quick temper, disloyalty and careless words. Conversely, relationships are enriched by patience, calmness, loyalty, good listening and carefully chosen words. It is the Spirit who grows in us the fruit needed to build our relationships – 'love, joy, peace, forbearance, kindness, goodness, faithfulness, gentleness and self-control' (Galatians 5:22–23).

Relationships are important for our enjoyment and well-being, as well as for our survival. As a result of Covid-19, connecting with other people has been made harder, yet there has been an outpouring of kindness shown to the more vulnerable and isolated. We have discovered anew our interdependence. In the book *Together* (Profile Books/Wellcome Collection, 2020), Dr Vivek Murthy describes the presence of a 'global loneliness epidemic' resulting in many people struggling with mental health issues. This affects the young and the old, with anxiety and depression particularly increasing among teenage girls, sometimes linked to the overuse of social media, which connects and isolates simultaneously.

Lord, may we be loving people, remembering that 'love is patient, love is kind. It does not envy, it does not boast, it is not proud... It always protects, always trusts, always hopes, always perseveres. Love never fails'
(1 Corinthians 13:4, 7–8a).

FIONA STRATTA

Celebration

So I commend the enjoyment of life… Go, eat your food with gladness, and drink your wine with a joyful heart, for God has already approved what you do. Always be clothed in white, and always anoint your head with oil. Enjoy life with your wife, whom you love, all the days of this meaningless life that God has given you under the sun… So then, banish anxiety from your heart and cast off the troubles of your body.

The Teacher advocated a celebratory attitude towards life. He would have approved of the charge to 'seize the day' (*carpe diem*), penned by the poet Horace in 23BC. We have been urged to enjoy life – relationships, work, possessions, plans and activities; to take no one and nothing for granted; and to take time to celebrate. We rejoice in our blessings 'under the sun' *and* 'through the Son'.

For those of us who may feel uncomfortable when we are 'being' rather than 'doing', or slightly guilty when enjoying leisure, the Teacher gives us wonderful words of assurance: 'God has already approved of what you do.' God is for us! White clothes and heads anointed with oil were both signs that a person was celebrating. We can be realistic about life in the real world and yet still celebrate, says the Teacher, for we are in God's hands (9:1).

Let us return to our title: enjoying life with God in the real world. Each phrase is indispensable: 'enjoying life' – 'with God' – 'in the real world'. Many try to enjoy life in the real world but without any reference to God. The Teacher has shown this to be meaningless. Enjoying life with God but giving no attention to the real world with its uncertainties and injustices can leave us out of touch with the pain of others and unable to cope with major ebbs in our lives. Being with God in the real world but not knowing how to enjoy life is to fail to grasp that Jesus came to give us life to the full. So let us 'banish anxiety', 'cast off the troubles' of our bodies and enjoy life with God in the real world.

Lord, thank you that you are for us and that we are conquerors through Christ who loves us.

FIONA STRATTA

Heaven

When the author of Genesis begins by describing God creating the heavens and earth, we know something important is being marked. The scope of God's creative energy is being set out, so that readers and listeners understand that the sovereign Lord holds all things within his care. In these readings, we trace the way scripture develops the image of heaven as the place from which God extends his reign, sometimes dramatically with thunder and lightning, through to the astonishing claim of Jesus Christ that, supremely, he brings heaven to earth in his life, death and resurrection.

Even within the Old Testament we see how different understandings of heaven emerge and develop, illustrating how the faith of Israel expands to meet the God who is active in the life of his people. Solomon's great prayer dedicating the temple is such an example and a foil to any suggestion that God is confined to a locality or a particular way of ministering. The king's words might be heeded afresh today, because they refute all claims of absolute control: only God, whose glory cannot be contained by all the heavens, let alone the temple, holds sway over all that is, seen and unseen.

In the New Testament, the coming of Jesus is decisive in the way we understand what heaven means. We must abandon all thoughts that we are speaking about a fluffy cloud or someplace 'up there' with the apostle Peter as arbiter of our destiny. It is in Jesus' miracles and teaching and, supremely, in his death and resurrection that we see the kingdom present in all Jesus did. In other words, it is better to speak of heaven come to earth rather than heaven as the far-off, distant reality many dream of achieving, seldom realising the offer of eternity John describes so eloquently in his gospel.

Further reflections into the New Testament show how Jesus secures our place in the heavenly realms because our lives are now 'hidden' with him (Colossians 3:3) and it is impossible for us to be separated from the loving grip Jesus exercises (Romans 8:38–39) towards his own.

The emphasis across the testaments is that there is no limit to God's reign, offering hope but also challenge, because it is only from within a relationship with Jesus that these certainties are offered to us.

ANDY JOHN

In the beginning

In the beginning God created the heavens and the earth. Now the earth was formless and empty, darkness was over the surface of the deep, and the Spirit of God was hovering over the waters. And God said, 'Let there be light,' and there was light. God saw that the light was good, and he separated the light from the darkness. God called the light 'day', and the darkness he called 'night'. And there was evening, and there was morning – the first day.

The opening words of the Bible describe the beginning of all things. This beautiful piece of writing sets the tone for everything that will follow because it marks a starting point in the history of God's dealings with the world.

Whereas some have focused on the processes and timeline for this act of creation, the writer emphasises the range of God's sovereign control. The words 'the heavens and the earth' emphasise that everything has been created by God. There is no part of the creation that God has not made. It is possible this scripture became important in the life of God's people when they were facing a crisis of faith in Babylon, following the fall of Jerusalem in 587BC. When the world seemed full of disorder and chaos, it must have provided hope to hear again that God was lord of all things.

We might gloss over the words 'heaven and earth' and fail to grasp the writer's conviction that God is lord of all that is, both 'seen and unseen', as we affirm in the Nicene Creed. The phrase captures the conviction that God's reign extends over all creation. And such a faith finds a personal connection when we face uncertainty or chaos, such as bereavement or a sudden change in circumstances. It also has traction in the wider context of a society coming to terms with the Covid-19 pandemic. How we move beyond any crisis invites new engagement with this scripture, because it asserts that God is Lord of all.

Almighty God, you sustain everything by the power of your word.
May I find new faith in your sovereign power today and a steady confidence that you are Lord of all. Amen

ANDY JOHN

Heaven – the place of God

Isaac spoke up and said to his father Abraham, 'Father?' 'Yes, my son?' Abraham replied. 'The fire and wood are here,' Isaac said, 'but where is the lamb for the burnt offering?' Abraham answered, 'God himself will provide the lamb for the burnt offering, my son.' And the two of them went on together. When they reached the place God had told him about, Abraham built an altar there and arranged the wood on it. He bound his son Isaac and laid him on the altar, on top of the wood. Then he reached out his hand and took the knife to slay his son. But the angel of the Lord called out to him from heaven, 'Abraham! Abraham!' 'Here I am,' he replied.

The story of Abraham and Isaac is well known. No one who reads it can fail to be moved and astonished at the way the story develops: God calls Abraham to slay his son. Aside from the crisis this would create (how would God maintain his promise that all nations would be blessed through his offspring, if the son dies?), it also raises questions about the God who tests Abraham in this way. A context of other religions sanctioning child sacrifice does little to shift the unease we feel.

However, there is more to this story. The angel of the Lord, speaking the very words of God, calls out 'from heaven'. The location of God as the one who dwells in heaven tells us something we might easily miss. The gods of this period were often local, tribal deities – statues who could be controlled. They were called upon for protection and to bless the good fortune of the household.

But the God of Abraham is not some block of wood to be brought out when things are challenging! The Lord God is apart, in heaven, and not subject to human attempts to master the divine. Whenever we associate God too closely with our own ambitions and plans, we need this verse to remind us that we are the clay, God is the potter. Reigning from heaven, he is worthy of our every attention.

Lord God, set our sights on things above, where you reign,
Father, Son and Holy Spirit. Amen

ANDY JOHN

The highest heavens

'Now Lord, the God of Israel, keep for your servant David my father the promises you made to him when you said, "You shall never fail to have a successor to sit before me on the throne of Israel, if only your descendants are careful in all they do to walk before me faithfully as you have done." And now, God of Israel, let your word that you promised your servant David my father come true. But will God really dwell on earth? The heavens, even the highest heaven, cannot contain you. How much less this temple I have built!'

These verses are part of a long prayer offered by King Solomon. In the book of Kings and elsewhere Solomon is presented as a wise monarch whose insights allowed him to rule after his father David. His fame and fortune spread across the whole of the ancient Near East. Although his later rule was marred by oppressive taxation and some dubious moral choices, this prayer captures well the wisdom for which he is famous.

Solomon's prayer of dedication of the temple lifts our understanding above any notion that God is contained by human structure or institution. His rule from heaven shows that he is the Lord reigning over the creation, neither simply one with it nor so removed from it as to be like an absent landlord. Solomon's genius, however, was recognising that not only could the temple not contain God but neither could the heaven of heavens. He grasps something of the majesty and glory of God.

The vision offered to us in the New Testament is that God is able to do more than we ask or imagine (Ephesians 3:20). The God revealed to us in Jesus invites us to a faith that rises to meet the stature of his greatness. We easily shape and mould God in our own image and limit the extent of his reign by restraints of which we are often unaware. Today, this verse invites us to come and see the wonder and glory of God afresh.

Living Lord, give us the faith that, like Solomon, sees your true glory and greatness. May our vision of you inspire us to new faith and service for Jesus' sake. Amen

ANDY JOHN

Rending the heavens

Oh, that you would rend the heavens and come down, that the mountains would tremble before you! As when fire sets twigs ablaze and causes water to boil, come down to make your name known to your enemies and cause the nations to quake before you! For when you did awesome things that we did not expect, you came down, and the mountains trembled before you.

The latter part of the book of Isaiah is full of longing. The earlier vision and hope of a return for God's people, who were languishing in Babylon, seems to have dimmed. The expectation that a messiah-like figure would bring about lasting change in the fortunes of the Hebrews has refocused on the need for reform and repentance. Today's verse captures that longing in a powerful prayer rich in the symbolism of lightning storms and summer wildfires that consume all before them.

We might relate to this kind of prayer that calls God to step from that hidden realm to come to our aid quickly. We may also have prayed this prayer when in danger or threatened, or perhaps when deeply conscious of our human frailty. Here heaven represents the place in which God resides and from which he must move if there is to be blessing and encounter. The scriptures contain other occasions where something similar takes place. Paul's experience on the Damascus road might sit alongside this prayer.

Throughout the ages Christians have described experiences like this, both in the quiet and in the joyful exuberance of worship, when it feels as though the heavens really are rent and mountains quake. Julian of Norwich captured her intense visions in her *Revelations of Divine Love*, and John Wesley spoke about his heart being strangely warmed. What connects all of these is a reaching out for God, for a taste of heaven itself, and an expectation that God will be found.

Almighty God, we long for you and your all-consuming love. Reach out to us afresh today and may we draw near to you and experience the intensity of your presence. In Jesus' name. Amen

ANDY JOHN

The heavenly kingdom

In those days John the Baptist came, preaching in the wilderness of Judea and saying, 'Repent, for the kingdom of heaven has come near.' This is he who was spoken of through the prophet Isaiah: 'A voice of one calling in the wilderness, "Prepare the way for the Lord, make straight paths for him."'

In the gospels, the evangelists refer to 'the kingdom of God', and in Matthew, on occasions, to the 'kingdom of heaven'. It is clear the two are synonymous. What was extraordinary in the teaching of Jesus was that he both spoke about the coming of this kingdom and ushered it in through his own ministry, death and resurrection. When John the Baptist preached his message, he was signalling the arrival of Jesus the Messiah and all that would follow.

Any reading of Jesus' ministry will see what characterises this kingdom: it is the way God brings heaven to earth. We see it in the healing of the sick (Matthew 8:3), people being fed (Mark 6:41–42), the demonised released from their torment (Luke 8:29) and even the dead being raised (John 11:43–44). We see what life looks like when the reign and rule of God is present.

It is easy to picture heaven as some fluffy cloud on which angels harp their songs and where the apostle Peter waits at a gate to measure us up. In the gospels, by contrast, heaven looks decidedly earthy in its nature and how it challenges the patterns and priorities we hold. When Jesus brought this salvation from above, it was not always welcomed. Sometimes the very rich went away disconsolate (Matthew 19:22) and the disturbance to a local economy predicated on exploitation was strongly resisted (Mark 5:17).

When we work with God in bringing the kingdom of heaven to our churches, communities and nation, we are joining God in the very ministry he came to establish in Jesus. We need to pray and reflect on what this means for us and how we can respond to the reality that in Jesus, the kingdom of heaven has drawn near.

Lord Jesus, bring your kingdom in ways that touch the lives of others.
Give us opportunities to bless that inspire us to serve.
For your name's sake. Amen

ANDY JOHN

Falling from heaven

The seventy-two returned with joy and said, 'Lord, even the demons submit to us in your name.' He replied, 'I saw Satan fall like lightning from heaven. I have given you authority to trample on snakes and scorpions and to overcome all the power of the enemy; nothing will harm you. However, do not rejoice that the spirits submit to you, but rejoice that your names are written in heaven.'

We have already seen that the kingdom of heaven brought hope for the needy and poor. Jesus' ministry released the power of God in a new way into people's lives and opened fresh possibilities for them into the future. In today's verse we read something unexpected: Jesus, upon hearing how the kingdom was breaking out through the disciples' ministry, speaks of Satan's fall.

It is not important whether this is meant to be a figure of speech or more than that. What is important is how Jesus saw the kingdom of heaven rolling back the darkness of Satan's domain. This conflict between two kingdoms is peppered throughout the gospels and the New Testament. The in-breaking of God's kingdom directly confronted all that was opposed to God and resistant to his reign.

We experience this same conflict today whenever the gospel is preached, and we ought not to assume there will be universal applause when we address issues of injustice, inequality and sinful practices wherever they show themselves. It is also critical we know that God's power is greater than the forces of darkness (1 John 4:4). This struggle is not between equally matched forces, where the outcome is hard to call. This does not mean that we crusade and wield power as though we have some divine right to control all of life; rather, we join God in bringing justice and hope to a needy world, even when this is challenging. When we do this, we too should expect to see Satan fall from heaven.

Living God, the challenge of following you can be demanding when there is conflict. I feel more at home with the quiet and peaceful tasks of life. Help me to hold with courage the faith and life which bring an end to what is dark and despairing. In Jesus' name. Amen

ANDY JOHN

In paradise

But the other criminal rebuked him. 'Don't you fear God,' he said, 'since you are under the same sentence? We are punished justly, for we are getting what our deeds deserve. But this man has done nothing wrong.' Then he said, 'Jesus, remember me when you come into your kingdom.' Jesus answered him, 'Truly I tell you, today you will be with me in paradise.'

In my chapel at Bishop's House, above the vestry door I have a wood carving with the words of today's reading. Each time I leave the chapel I see these words and they never fail to move me. Although Jesus does not use the word 'heaven' explicitly, the idea is undoubtedly present in his use of the word 'paradise'.

We are at the most profound moment in the gospels: Jesus is crucified and soon he will 'breathe his last' (Luke 23:46) and die. Two criminals will suffer the same fate, but they regard this and their relationship to Jesus quite differently. One pours out his scorn and rage at this bitter end; the other casts himself, figuratively, on Jesus' care and kindness. This second criminal turns his request into a kind of prayer. He has nothing Jesus needs, has nothing to offer and brings no excuse nor lame explanation. His request is to be with Jesus in the life to come.

The word Jesus uses, rarely employed in the New Testament, sums up the offer of life. We should avoid any suggestion that paradise is equated with a life of unchecked feasting. What is offered is Jesus' presence, the lover of our souls in whom we live and for whom we were made. And such a gift is his to give when we reach out, much like the words in that loved hymn 'Rock of Ages': 'Nothing in my hand I bring, simply to thy cross I cling' (Augustus Toplady, 1763).

When Christians understand that they are entirely loved by God and need offer nothing save to accept the grace offered, they are like that thief, invited to come home to paradise.

Lord Jesus, you opened wide your arms of love on the cross
to welcome a criminal and all who turn to you. Praise and adoration
to you now and always. Amen

ANDY JOHN

Heavenly bread

Jesus said to them, 'Very truly I tell you, it is not Moses who has given you the bread from heaven, but it is my Father who gives you the true bread from heaven. For the bread of God is the bread that comes down from heaven and gives life to the world.' 'Sir,' they said, 'always give us this bread.' Then Jesus declared, 'I am the bread of life. Whoever comes to me will never go hungry, and whoever believes in me will never be thirsty.'

We can imagine the disciples knew what the smell of bread was like: freshly baked, straight from the oven. Bread from heaven must have sounded better still: an endless supply, forever fresh and baked to perfection. At the very moment when they might have been salivating, Jesus shifts the image unexpectedly: to himself, the true bread from heaven who gives life to the world.

We use the phrase 'heavenly' in our everyday conversations for something especially nice. When Jesus describes himself as bread from heaven, it cannot only mean where he came from. The invitation Jesus makes is to discover the riches and treasures of heaven in him. A prayer attributed to Augustine captures the longing in our hearts for more than the material things of life: 'Thou hast formed us for thyself, and our hearts are restless till they find rest in thee.' The gospel is all too often imagined as a chore or a task, whereas it is first and foremost the offer Jesus makes to give us a life that is richer by far than anything we could manufacture.

An image from many years ago is indelibly stuck in my mind. It is of a whole town rummaging through the city's rubbish tip searching for scraps. It is of course a dreadful indictment of a world of plenty that any person should be reduced to scavenging. But this is sometimes true spiritually too. We content ourselves on the crumbs, when Jesus offers the food from heaven which meets our deepest needs and satisfies our souls.

Lord Jesus, our hearts are restless and we long for food that fills us.
Give us this bread from heaven, now and always. Amen

ANDY JOHN

This same Jesus

After he said this, he was taken up before their very eyes, and a cloud hid him from their sight. They were looking intently up into the sky as he was going, when suddenly two men dressed in white stood beside them. 'Men of Galilee,' they said, 'why do you stand here looking into the sky? This same Jesus, who has been taken from you into heaven, will come back in the same way you have seen him go into heaven.'

When the angels addressed the disciples, I wonder if there was a sense of déjà vu? Those who had run to the grave, finding it empty, also found themselves addressed by heavenly visitors. These messengers from above announce the deep things of heaven, underlining the significance of what others are witnessing. And so it is here: angels make known the purpose of God in the ascension of Jesus to the place he came from.

Of course, we can wrongly imagine heaven is up there above the clouds. Famously and with irony, the Russian astronaut Yuri Gagarin peered from his spacecraft and said, 'I don't see any God up here.' The ascension of Jesus, however, marks his return to the Father and the establishment of his reign as victorious king. Without the ascension and start of this reign, the Holy Spirit would not have been sent, poured out on all believers so that heaven's power could be released on earth. As Jesus came from the 'realms of glory', it was fitting he should return there, so that the new era of God being present across time and space rather than limited to a single country could begin.

The angels have one more piece to add to this significant message: as Jesus ascended to the Father, it is from there that he shall return to complete what began in Bethlehem. His heavenly reign will one day overlap entirely with the physical world and Christ will be all in all. As we affirm confidently in the Nicene Creed, 'He will come again in glory to judge the living and the dead.'

Lord Jesus, you reign in heaven and on earth. May your reign be extended from there across all nations. Amen

ANDY JOHN

Clothed with immortality

For we know that if the earthly tent we live in is destroyed, we have a building from God, an eternal house in heaven, not built by human hands. Meanwhile we groan, longing to be clothed instead with our heavenly dwelling, because when we are clothed, we will not be found naked. For while we are in this tent, we groan and are burdened, because we do not wish to be unclothed but to be clothed instead with our heavenly dwelling, so that what is mortal may be swallowed up by life.

Stuart was a skilled climber and knew how to look after himself, even in the winter months on the slopes of Snowdonia. But nothing would have prepared him for the ferocity of the storm that broke upon him and his friends some years ago. Their tent was torn apart and discarded, and they were left to huddle together, hoping the dawn would allow a descent to safety. At the height of the storm, the words of our reading came to him: 'If this tent is destroyed, we have a building from God, an eternal house in heaven.'

Paul's contrast of the earthly tent with the house in heaven opens one of the great themes in the New Testament. Christians have not always agreed how this promise should be understood, but there can be no doubting the direction it sets: in Christ we are safe. And this confidence is not ours because we are the guarantors of this trust, but because God is faithful. There is never any suggestion that this allows us to rest on our laurels. Far from it. It was confidence in the mercy of God that inspired the first Christians in the Jerusalem church to become witnesses of the resurrection and life of God, even when doing so was to their detriment.

This kind of security ought to liberate us from a fearful serving of God into one in which his love compels us to live and walk in the footsteps of the early Christians. Stuart discovered something profound that day, and the story invites us to that same confidence.

Lord Jesus, in you we find our security. Help us to live in this each day. Amen

ANDY JOHN

Inexpressible things

And I know that this man… was caught up to paradise and heard inexpressible things, things that no one is permitted to tell. I will boast about a man like that, but I will not boast about myself, except about my weaknesses… But I refrain, so no one will think more of me than is warranted by what I do or say, or because of these surpassingly great revelations. Therefore, in order to keep me from becoming conceited, I was given a thorn in my flesh.

The encounter Paul describes in our reading for today is unlike almost any other in the New Testament. It is not absolutely clear whether Paul is speaking of his own experience, although I think this is likely, even if he claims he will not boast about himself. Whether Paul or a fellow Christian, it seems an encounter so intense and powerful was experienced that it felt, and may have actually been, as though in heaven.

We may have read books outside the New Testament in which similar things are thought to have occurred. However we understand these, my own view is that sometimes the Lord does give these moments of such closeness that it seems we are surrounded by heaven. I confess I am not sure whether these moments are mostly in order to prepare us for something we might face or simply because the Lord parts the clouds out of his great love. Possibly it is both of these. I am more sure, however, that we should learn to long for God with greater fervour and perseverance. When he becomes our deepest desire, this in itself lifts us and draws us more deeply into his love.

What is significant in the reading is how God provides an antidote to any boasting! If the experience might puff us up, the thorns keep us rooted in the everyday consciousness of our weakness, sin and everlasting need of God. Here we discover something profound: in order to do God's work, we need something of heaven and earth, not the one or the other.

Lord Jesus Christ, draw me deeper into an experience of you, so that I may love you more and learn how to live your life here on earth. Amen

ANDY JOHN

To die is gain

I eagerly expect and hope that I will in no way be ashamed, but will have sufficient courage so that now as always Christ will be exalted in my body, whether by life or by death. For to me, to live is Christ and to die is gain. If I am to go on living in the body, this will mean fruitful labour for me. Yet what shall I choose? I do not know! I am torn between the two: I desire to depart and be with Christ, which is better by far; but it is more necessary for you that I remain in the body.

When Paul wrote this letter, it is likely that he was in a Roman jail. His cell would have been small, and he might have been restrained within the cell itself. Some of the letter is dedicated to the way God overcomes obstacles and even makes hindrances the means by which God opens new doors for the gospel. Early in the letter, Paul contemplates the possibility that he might never leave. But his anguish is not that he might be executed but rather the conflict of wanting to be with Christ when he knows it might be better if he stays alive.

Paul's conviction is that, were he to die, he would go to be with Christ directly. When he met Jesus on the road to Damascus, everything changed. He became convinced that Jesus was Lord and that he and all God's people would spend eternity with him on his return or through death and entry to heaven.

Christians have not been sure whether this passing into Christ's presence is immediate (although that is my view) or whether we sleep and at the resurrection enter consciously into paradise. The important thing is that this was no fearful passing to be regarded with dread. And that is the invitation made to us, too. Whereas many would find the end of life despairing to contemplate, for Christians it is the means by which we meet our friend and Saviour face to face.

Lord Jesus, you give me assurance that you will not abandon me in death, and so I believe. Praise and honour to you. Amen

ANDY JOHN

Hidden with Christ

So if you have been raised with Christ, seek the things that are above, where Christ is, seated at the right hand of God. Set your minds on things that are above, not on things that are on earth, for you have died, and your life is hidden with Christ in God. When Christ who is your life is revealed, then you also will be revealed with him in glory.

In today's reading, we see how Paul invites the Colossian Christians to align their lives to the reality of our situation in Christ. If our lives are hidden with him in God, we ought to live as people of heaven. Throughout the New Testament, we see how the resurrection of Jesus places him at the heart of God's glorious reign. In Revelation, the victory of Jesus becomes the music of heaven (5:11–12) and invites the adoration of angels. Because Jesus is at the right hand of God and we are grafted into him, our lives must now be oriented towards reflecting his reign.

Here lies one of the most beautiful truths for all Christians. In the Lord's Prayer we pray that the kingdom might come, perhaps seldom grasping that it does so through us! As we align ourselves to God, it is by our lives that something of heaven is not only revealed but created. We become the means by which God brings heaven to earth. And the importance of this is that it lifts those acts which seem random and insignificant to a higher level. The act of kindness, the word of encouragement, the persevering in love – these might seem without consequence, but I am sure they are the way that God brings heaven to earth.

The challenge we face is one in which we seek to work with God faithfully and humbly, attending to those 'small things' commended by the Welsh saint David, who saw that the accumulation of these acts was not just a matter of being good, still less of notching up points, but the way in which we share in the transformation of the whole world.

Lord, help us to see our lives in the light of what you are doing
in Jesus. Amen

ANDY JOHN

A new heaven

Then I saw 'a new heaven and a new earth,' for the first heaven and the first earth had passed away, and there was no longer any sea. I saw the Holy City, the new Jerusalem, coming down out of heaven from God, prepared as a bride beautifully dressed for her husband. And I heard a loud voice from the throne saying, 'Look! God's dwelling-place is now among the people, and he will dwell with them. They will be his people, and God himself will be with them and be their God.'

Fans of the 1997 film *Titanic* will know how a sermon based on the words of today's passage is preached as the boat begins its slow descent into the icy waters of the Atlantic. Only slightly less familiar than the quartet playing 'Nearer my God to thee', the legend is probably greater than the reality but captures the sense of impending doom that awaits the ocean-going liner.

The vision John describes in our reading today is powerful and provides an appropriate comparison with the opening words of Genesis 1. This new heaven and earth mark a conclusion to the letter he has been crafting. All the world's tribulations, and especially those of the church, are gathered into this act of creation by the one who is Lord of all. The imagery is familiar ('the new Jerusalem', for example) but dramatic, because it describes the end of the old order and the beginning of something new.

We might have seen or heard street preachers making a big deal of texts like this and been astonished at how lurid the descriptions are. But John's words ought not to be taken in this way. Rather they are showing how God's future, secured in Christ, is wonderfully and radically different from all that has been until now. How God will achieve this is less important than the fact that it is within God's sovereign control alone. In other words, this reinforces the author's conviction that all history and all created things are within his care as Saviour and judge. This is offered not to scare, but to invite faith.

Living God, author and Lord of all, to you only we entrust ourselves,
for you sustain and reign over all. Amen

ANDY JOHN

1 and 2 Thessalonians

 Some scholars believe 1 Thessalonians to be Paul's first letter, which would make it among the very earliest documents in the New Testament. The newness of the Christian church that is being addressed here is startling. These Christians were probably only a few months old, spiritually speaking. Here is a new society in the making; an experiment in a radically different way of being. This makes these letters a vital witness to what it means to live in the midst of a world that does not know Christ. They also offer insight into the importance of seeking wise guides and not being afraid to ask for help.

From Paul's point of view, we see a mature teacher who is never impatient with questions or tempted to put people down because they have got hold of the wrong end of the stick. No doubt he had taught them about the promised return of the risen Jesus, but they had quickly worked themselves into a state of confusion over it, as these letters demonstrate.

Ideas about the shape of the resurrection life are as confusing today as they were in the first century AD. Christians have argued over every aspect of the Lord's return and if we imagine that somewhere there is a precise blueprint, we have missed the point. Instead, we are given what we need to know and how we should live in the light of it. Jesus told his followers he would come back and instructed them what to do in the meantime. Every time we pray 'Your kingdom come', we join those Thessalonians and all believers since then who eagerly looked forward to the Lord's return.

Christians believe the new age of the reign of God on earth has begun in Jesus, but we still await its coming in fullness. The message of these two letters is that what will be in the future must shape what we are now. Christian hope illuminates how we live in the present. There is a sense in which Christianity is a waiting game. It is how we wait that counts. As Paul wrote, 'May the Master take you by the hand and lead you along the path of God's love and Christ's endurance' (2 Thessalonians 3:5, MSG).

LIZ HOARE

Thanksgiving

Paul, Silvanus and Timothy, To the church of the Thessalonians in God the Father and the Lord Jesus Christ: Grace to you and peace. We always give thanks to God for all of you and mention you in our prayers, constantly remembering before our God and Father your work of faith and labour of love and steadfastness of hope in our Lord Jesus Christ.

Grace and peace are two profoundly Christian attributes that stem directly from the character of God himself. Throughout the Bible, we see the grace of God at work over and over again, supremely in the way that God came to dwell among us as a vulnerable human being. The peace of God, as Paul says elsewhere, 'passes all [human] understanding' and is only found in God. It is this peace that 'keep[s] our hearts and minds in the knowledge and love of God', as Anglicans hear in the blessing at the end of every Communion service.

These are the precious gifts that Paul longs to be experienced by the readers of these two short letters. They are full of warmth and encouragement that give rise to deep thanksgiving. It has not been long since he was experiencing their faith, love and hope for himself. We might imagine him explaining to them what grace looks like from God's perspective and then how they could experience it in their own lives through the love of the Lord Jesus. This was indeed good news and the Thessalonian Christians were those who had received it gladly and committed themselves to living it out. Paul had to leave them, trusting that grace would keep them and remembering their work of faith, labour of love and steadfastness of hope as evidence that the seed he had sown had begun to grow.

What would this kind of faith, love and hope look like in our communities today? Examples of Christians demonstrating these characteristics during the pandemic abounded: praying for streets and communities, social media groups for encouragement and support, food banks and everyday caring for neighbours.

Are there people in our lives for whom we are constantly thankful, who demonstrate faith, hope and love that radiates out to others? Pray for them.

LIZ HOARE

Word and power

For we know, brothers and sisters beloved by God, that he has chosen you, because our message of the gospel came to you not in word only, but also in power and in the Holy Spirit and with full conviction; just as you know what kind of people we proved to be among you for your sake.

All words, and faith soon grows dry and cerebral. All Spirit, and it becomes all too easy to drift away into subjective feelings. Word and Spirit together, on the other hand, equal supernatural dynamite.

We know from his letters that Paul understood the power of oratory. He could argue and persuade along with the rest, but his preaching and writing alone could not lead to spiritual awakening and new life. Paul is in no doubt that the Thessalonians have been transformed by the gospel. 'We know,' he says, that the gospel has taken root in good soil and is bearing fruit. These dear people have been chosen and have responded accordingly. This is not all their own doing, of course. God's grace, as the opening words note, is at the heart of their transformation. The gospel has taken root through the word preached and demonstrated in the power of the Holy Spirit to bring about a thorough conversion.

The relationship Paul and his fellow leaders have with the Thessalonians is reciprocal, too, for they have also proved themselves when living among them. It was never about superior leaders laying heavy burdens on vulnerable people that they themselves were unwilling to shoulder. The letter goes on to emphasise how, at every stage, Paul lived out what he was preaching and never asked anything of his converts that he was not willing to do himself.

Paul's confidence in the Thessalonian church is an encouragement in itself. Have you ever had someone believe in you to the extent that it influenced your performance? Sportsmen and women often say that it is the cheering of the crowds that line the track that drives them on to win more than anything else.

Pray for someone who needs encouragement today,
then be an encouragement to them in some way.

LIZ HOARE

An example

And you became imitators of us and of the Lord, for in spite of persecution you received the word with joy inspired by the Holy Spirit, so that you became an example to all the believers in Macedonia and in Achaia. For the word of the Lord has sounded forth from you not only in Macedonia and Achaia, but in every place where your faith in God has become known.

It's a brave church leader (or an arrogant one) who tells their congregation to imitate them! Here Paul seems to go even further by bracketing his own example with the Lord himself. Happily, we know enough about Paul from his letters to know that he sat lightly to his earthly successes, which were many, and was humble in his demeanour towards the churches in his care. We also know that his meeting with the risen Lord Jesus on the Damascus Road had turned his life inside out and all his values now looked different.

What is more, Paul had endured persecution, and we discover that the Thessalonians had too. Their character, like his, was shaped by suffering. It is this that enables him to place himself in the same breath as his Lord, who for our sake endured the cross. Paul was sharing in the sufferings of Christ and that gave him authority to write as he does here.

The surprise comes as Paul singles out 'joy' as describing the way the Thessalonians came to faith. Paul often referred to joy in his letters, even from his prison cell (Philippians), and joy is another characteristic of the indwelling of the Holy Spirit. It is also the way that Jesus himself went to the cross (Hebrews 12:2). Paul, the Thessalonians and the Lord Jesus are held together in fellowship and spiritual bonds that go deep. Of course, with such responsibility for the churches in his care, Paul as leader was open to temptations to abuse his authority, just as leaders are today.

Pray for God's protection for those appointed over you in your church, especially if they have a wider profile in the public domain. And pray too for churches seeking new leadership, that they will find people who combine spiritual gifts with humility and dependence on the Holy Spirit.

LIZ HOARE

Forsaken

O Lord, all my longing is known to you; my sighing is not hidden from you. My heart throbs, my strength fails me; as for the light of my eyes – it also has gone from me. My friends and companions stand aloof from my affliction, and my neighbours stand far off… Do not forsake me, O Lord; O my God do not be far from me; make haste to help me, O Lord, my salvation.

Psalm 38 is a psalm of penitence and a plea for forgiveness and healing. It is a fitting psalm for Ash Wednesday, then, but there is more. Sin cuts us off from God and, as he confesses his wrongdoing, the psalmist also expresses his fear that God will rebuke him in his anger and abandon him to his plight. Sin also cuts us off from one another, and the sense of isolation is palpable here. Friends, companions and neighbours all stand far off, reluctant to have anything to do with him in his grief and regret. In this psalm, it seems that some so-called friends are even out to trip him up and expose him further. Who can help him? At last he realises where his true hope lies: 'It is for you O Lord, that I wait; it is you, O Lord my God, who will answer' (v. 15).

As much as we talk about the fresh start that God gives to us when we confess our sins, we are not always so forgiving towards sinners ourselves, preferring to keep them at arm's length. Lent is an invitation to recognise our common need of mercy. All of us stand far off until our sin is confessed, and God in his mercy brings us home.

This Lent many will feel isolation for other reasons than a specific wrongdoing. The Thessalonians felt abandoned because of persecution; others have felt cut off from family and loved ones, unable to give and receive a hug or the warmth of human presence. The words of this psalm speak to this kind of isolation, too. All of us, whatever our situation, can make the words of this psalm our own in times of need.

'O God, make speed to save us, O Lord, make haste to help us'
(Book of Common Prayer, 1662).

LIZ HOARE

Transparency in evangelism

Though we had already suffered and been shamefully maltreated at Philippi, as you know, we had courage in our God to declare to you the gospel of God in spite of great opposition. For our appeal does not spring from deceit or impure motives or trickery, but just as we have been approved by God to be entrusted with the message of the gospel, even so we speak.

Everyone loves the kind of stories where the heroine or hero suffers one setback after another only to carry on with courage and determination. Paul had setbacks enough and to spare, but God's gift of courage spurred him on to tell more and more people about Jesus. Paul had been beaten and imprisoned in Philippi for supposedly seditious teaching and might have taken a long break from his mission tours to recover. Instead, he arrived in Thessalonica to face yet more opposition as he persisted in talking about Jesus. He reminds the Thessalonians that he never tried to pull the wool over their eyes regarding his calling or used underhand means to trick them into believing him.

We still value people who speak and live with integrity today, and it is a vital part of the church's witness if we are to be heard among the myriad philosophies, lifestyles and promises of nirvana that are being peddled in so many quarters across the globe. What Paul needed, and what Christian witness continues to need, is courage. What did 'courage in our God' look like for Paul then, and what would it look like for you as you seek to live with integrity now?

Lord, give me courage once more for today. Amen

LIZ HOARE

Our joy and crown

As for us, brothers and sisters, when, for a short time, we were made orphans by being separated from you – in person, not in heart – we longed with great eagerness to see you face to face. For we wanted to come to you – certainly I, Paul, wanted to again and again – but Satan blocked our way. For what is our hope or joy or crown of boasting before our Lord Jesus at his coming? Is it not you? Yes, you are our glory and joy!

How the longing for a face-to-face meeting has resonated in the troubled days of the pandemic, with isolation for so many. It echoes Paul's anguish at not being able to see his new family. So much part of a new family were they that he felt as if he had been orphaned by their separation. For many people, the enforced absence from Christian fellowship was harsh and, like Paul, they felt a strong force not of good, important though keeping safe might be, but of evil keeping them apart.

But Paul cannot be downcast for long. As he thinks about their beloved faces, he exclaims that the Thessalonian Christians are his joy and crown. Is there an implicit message here? Persecution may have led to the Thessalonians feeling rejection, even abandonment, but Paul reassures them that acceptance by God leads to acceptance by others. He is ready to boast about them, his hope, glory and crown. He is looking forward to presenting them before King Jesus himself with joy.

Thank you, Lord Jesus, for my brothers and sisters whom you love and who bring you joy. Amen

LIZ HOARE

The encouragement of good news

But Timothy has just now come to us from you, and has brought us the good news of your faith and love. He has told us also that you always remember us kindly and long to see us – just as we long to see you. For this reason, brothers and sisters, during all our distress and persecution we have been encouraged about you through your faith.

Many of us who have moved away from a strong community of believers can empathise with Paul's longing to see his spiritual family again. In a very short time these people have become that dear to him.

It is true that deep bonds of affection can be formed very quickly. Christians have an immediate connection when they meet another believer, for we are together members of the body of Christ. Although Paul did not stay long in Thessalonica, perhaps only a few weeks, there was an immediate bond formed that left him longing to hear news of them. It seems the Thessalonians were used by God to build Paul up again after his battering at Philippi. The kind of news he was hoping for was about their faith, and Timothy brought that news. Their faith and love, along with their desire to see Paul as much as he desired to see them, were the important things. Notice how it is this rather than any worldly successes that encourages him so much.

Pray for those who mean a great deal to you in your Christian journey and, if possible, write one of them a note of encouragement today.

LIZ HOARE

Paul's prayer for the Thessalonians

Now may our God and Father himself and our Lord Jesus direct our way to you. And may the Lord make you increase and abound in love for one another and for all, just as we abound in love for you. And may he so strengthen your hearts in holiness that you may be blameless before our God and Father at the coming of our Lord Jesus with all his saints.

This is a deeply heartfelt prayer being uttered by the apostle Paul. He is often regarded as a prickly character, writing letters of correction. But it's clear from this letter that what meant most to him were the strong bonds of human affection grounded in the love of Christ.

Determined to keep seeking a way to see them again, Paul prays a prayer that encompasses their lives now and for all eternity. It is as if he is saying that love is the comprehensive grace in which all the others are included. We can never have too much of love for one another, for loving bears witness to Christ in us.

Paul wants the Thessalonians to be like an inexhaustible fountain overflowing with love. God is the source of this fountain of love which extends to us, too, as fellow believers in him. It is out of such love that holiness springs, love that is the fulfilment of the law.

Paul prays all this against the backdrop of Jesus coming again to gather up all things to himself. Such hope sets us free to love and to grow in holiness of heart.

Lord, may the fountain of your love overflow in me. Amen

LIZ HOARE

Keep doing what you are doing

Finally, brothers and sisters, we ask and urge you in the Lord Jesus that, as you learned from us how you ought to live and to please God (as, in fact, you are doing), you should do so more and more. For you know what instructions we gave you through the Lord Jesus. For this is the will of God, your sanctification.

'Just keep on doing the same thing' could sound like a recipe for a plodding existence, but that's not how we are to read Paul's instructions here. It is more like the invitation to join an eternal dance that weaves and dips in ever-changing patterns that always remain true to the rhythm of the tune. Are you working hard at loving? Keep at it. Do you pray for daily strength to grow in holiness? Keep on praying and practising. Do you remind one another what was said when I was with you and how I urged you to imitate me? Well, don't forget but keep reminding each other.

Chapter 4 does indeed go on to reiterate some very practical instructions Paul had passed on when he was with the Thessalonians from the teaching of Jesus. It's right that we are reminded of the practicalities of faith, hope and love in our daily lives. We may recall that this section of the letter follows Paul's prayer that the Thessalonians will continue to grow in holiness. God works his work of grace in us, and we are to work with God in working it out in our personal lives and situations.

Meditate on the words: 'This is the will of God, your sanctification.'

LIZ HOARE

The question of those who have died

But we do not want you to be uninformed, brothers and sisters, about those who have died, so that you may not grieve as others do who have no hope. For since we believe that Jesus died and rose again, even so, through Jesus, God will bring with him those who have died. For this we declare to you by the word of the Lord, that we who are alive, who are left until the coming of the Lord, will by no means precede those who have died… Therefore encourage one another with these words.

One big issue had arisen since Paul had moved on from Thessalonica. He had taught them to expect the imminent return of the Lord Jesus. It was a key part of their faith, perhaps all the more so because of persecution. But some of their number had died and Jesus had not yet come back. What would happen to them? They were afraid that these sisters and brothers would miss out.

Here Paul seeks to both reassure and correct misunderstanding. He stresses that Jesus will bring with him those who have died. They will in fact be the first to experience the resurrection for themselves.

Notice that Paul doesn't tell them not to grieve at all when loved ones die, but only not to grieve as those who have no hope. How important it was that their confusion had come to Paul's attention and that he was able to teach them the truth. And how thankful we may be today that we too may read God's truth in his word.

'Everyone who believes in him may not perish but may have eternal life'
(John 3:16b).

LIZ HOARE

Be watchful and alert

But you, beloved, are not in darkness, for that day to surprise you like a thief; for you are all children of light and children of the day; we are not of the night or of darkness. So then, let us not fall asleep as others do, but let us keep awake and be sober; for those who sleep sleep at night, and those who are drunk get drunk at night.

There are echoes of Jesus' parables here. He talked about thieves coming without warning and about staying awake and being watchful (the wise and foolish maidens, for example). He also referred to himself, and to his followers also, as 'the light of the world' (John 8:12; Matthew 5:14). So for Paul to remind his readers that they are children of light helps them reset their spiritual compass.

Light and dark have a double meaning here. To be in the dark could mean to be ignorant of what will happen, and they are fully aware (5:1–2). Dark could also mean moral darkness, but this is no longer the case, for God has shined his light into their hearts. As children of light, they won't be taken by surprise on 'the day of the Lord' as long as they live accordingly.

As children of light, we too are to keep awake and sober, meaning that we live in the light of the hope of Christ's return. This hope fills every present moment and frees us to respond to God's guiding Spirit in our lives.

Lord, help me to be watchful and alert to your Spirit today. Amen

LIZ HOARE

Final instructions

Be at peace among yourselves. And we urge you, beloved, to admonish the idlers, encourage the faint-hearted, help the weak, be patient with all of them. See that none of you repays evil for evil, but always seek to do good to one another and to all. Rejoice always, pray without ceasing, give thanks in all circumstances; for this is the will of God in Christ Jesus for you.

A cascade of final instructions flows from Paul's pen. This is how God wants the Thessalonians – and us – to live. Each little phrase demands careful attention.

Be at peace among yourselves needs constant repetition, for Christians seem so prone to quarrelling. 'Be at peace,' said one early Christian saint, 'and thousands around you will find salvation.' There are warnings here for those who have downed tools in anticipation of Christ's return, and a stern command not to seek vengeance.

Many early characteristics of the Christian church were, like the teachings of Jesus, deeply countercultural and marked out believers from those around them. The weak, for example, were viewed as people to be despised, but Paul urges the Thessalonians to look out specially for them.

He ends with three imperatives that have threaded this letter from beginning to end. Joy and rejoicing are the constants of Paul's demeanour towards them. Prayer is the air he breathes as he writes, and thanksgiving sets the tone of everything these people mean to him and he to them. All of these things together are the will of God for all whose lives are bound up with Christ Jesus.

Take one of these commands and make it your prayer throughout today.

LIZ HOARE

Did we miss it?

As to the coming of our Lord Jesus Christ and our being gathered together to him, we beg you, brothers and sisters, not to be quickly shaken in mind or alarmed, either by spirit or by word or by letter, as though from us, to the effect that the day of the Lord is already here. Let no one deceive you in any way.

Here we are again, with the Thessalonians worrying about Christ's second coming and Paul writing to reassure them. But the apostle is not irritated by their anxiety. The second letter begins with the same warmth as the first, with thanksgiving and joy, and the tone towards these young believers is now pastoral and concerned.

It seems that false teachers were undermining their confidence by saying that Christ had already returned and they had missed him! Paul tells them clearly that the Lord had not come yet, whatever anyone might say. This is the great lesson of this brief letter, written not long after the first. He goes on to explain that there will be a clear sequence of events, though there is no hint of dates or encouragement to guess when it will be.

The second coming has divided Christians since and distracted the church from what really matters – how we are to live in the in-between times. The two certainties noted here are that he will return and that believers will be gathered to him, never to be parted. New Christians may need their confidence building, while older ones may need jaded hopes renewed.

Give thanks for the assurance of the hope of Christ's return.

LIZ HOARE

Pray for us

Finally, brothers and sisters, pray for us, so that the word of the Lord may spread rapidly and be glorified everywhere, just as it is among you, and that we may be rescued from wicked and evil people; for not all have faith. But the Lord is faithful; he will strengthen you and guard you from the evil one. And we have confidence in the Lord concerning you.

Paul's letters to the Thessalonians are saturated with prayer, but it is not all one-way. Here he asks them to pray for him. What do we ask for when we request prayer for ourselves? Paul asks his beloved friends to pray and encourages them in Christ. He longs for the same kind of faith he can see in the Thessalonians to be spread abroad. He knows there is opposition and that obstacles to the work of the gospel will arise. He has no wish for anything for himself except to be kept from evil, so that the word of the Lord can do its work.

The foundation of all our praying is the faithfulness of the Lord, and here Paul once more reassures these young believers, telling them that the Lord will strengthen them for whatever comes. Paul keeps on pointing them away from the troubles surrounding them towards the God who is eternally faithful. He has taught them about the love of God and the endurance of the Lord Jesus and never pretends that the Christian life is easy. 'But the Lord is faithful.'

Thank you, Lord, that you are faithful.
Strengthen me to live for you each day. Amen

LIZ HOARE

Rest and recreation

I had to smile one day while visiting a convent kitchen. A fridge magnet was on prominent display, announcing to the sisters that 'Jesus is coming – Look busy!'

Many of us will, in the course of our working lives, have felt it necessary to speed up whatever we were doing when the boss showed up. I even knew a young wife once who, wanting to give her husband the impression that she had been hard at work all day, sprayed furniture polish on the radiator to produce the aroma of fresh housekeeping with rather less effort. My elders used to call this hard effort 'elbow grease', as they laboured to keep their homes spotless and dust-free.

It's hardly surprising that we might feel shocked into activity at the words 'Jesus is coming'. This reaction may be rooted in our assumption that God is some kind of taskmaster who expects us to pull our weight in the vineyard and earn our entrance to heaven. Yet in our hearts, as well as from scripture, we know that the truth is very different, and that in the divine dispensation everything is grace.

During the coming two weeks we will reflect on God's invitation to be less concerned about 'earning our keep' and more ready to rest in God's presence. It isn't easy to set aside our compulsion to be 'doing'. It has been laid upon us mainly by human, not divine, hands, beginning in childhood.

We begin our journey by hearing God's command to 'Stop!' echoing down the ages. If this command is difficult to take on board, we then go on to see how Jesus sets us an example of what it means to come to rest, and asks us to do likewise. Our inner Martha wants to fix things in the kitchen; our inner Mary is drawn to sit at Jesus' feet. We go on to learn from him how to handle stormy waters by resting at the still centre.

We are not left without practical guidance, however. It can be hard to switch off our busyness, but scripture can help us as we are gently guided to the inner space, where all that is asked of us is that we let the face of God shine upon us and bless us.

MARGARET SILF

Stop!

Remember the sabbath day and keep it holy. For six days you shall labour and do all your work. But the seventh day is a sabbath to the Lord your God; you shall not do any work… For in six days the Lord made heaven and earth, the sea, and all that is in them, but rested the seventh day; therefore the Lord blessed the sabbath day and consecrated it… When you enter the land that I am giving you, the land shall observe a sabbath for the Lord. For six years you shall sow your field, and for six years you shall prune your vineyard… but in the seventh year there shall be a sabbath of complete rest for the land.

How often have you heard it said of someone – or perhaps of yourself – 'They never stop'? Indeed, there are those who take positive pride in never giving themselves a break. It's so easy, in today's driven, pressured world, to forget that, as the saying goes, we are first and foremost human beings, not human doings.

The intuition that this is not the right way to live is articulated in the first part of today's reading, where God breaks right through all our busyness and says, quite simply, 'Stop!' This isn't just a piece of friendly advice. It's a command. It spells out clearly that both our physical and our spiritual well-being depend on regularly pausing our frantic activity and ensuring that our lifestyle leaves others free to take their own rest and recreation.

In the second part of the reading, we learn that this command also extends to the land – to the Earth. During the Covid-19 pandemic and the resulting global shutdown, with all its hardship, you could nevertheless almost hear the Earth sighing in relief, to be freed of our noise, stress and pollution, as though creation had had enough of our misbehaviour and sent us all to our rooms to reflect on our conduct. God's stop sign, however, isn't a punishment but a gift – the gift of regular rest for us and for our Earth, a gift which we neglect at our extreme peril.

Sabbath time takes many different forms. What form does it take for you?

MARGARET SILF

Doing and being

Now as they went on their way, he entered a certain village, where a woman named Martha welcomed him into her home. She had a sister named Mary, who sat at the Lord's feet and listened to what he was saying. But Martha was distracted by her many tasks; so she came to him and asked, 'Lord, do you not care that my sister has left me to do all the work by myself? Tell her then to help me.' But the Lord answered her, 'Martha, Martha, you are worried and distracted by many things; there is need of only one thing. Mary has chosen the better part, which will not be taken away from her.'

Yesterday we reflected on the God-given command to observe sabbath time in our lives. But God knows we are human and don't always do as we are told. Sometimes we can be perversely resistant to the force of a command, however needful that command may be to our well-being. Today, we hear the same message from God, but in the familiar setting of a friendly home. It's the same message but in a gentler, though equally uncompromising, form, as Jesus urges Martha to pause in her busyness and sit at his feet instead. Mary is so attracted to the love and wisdom of Jesus that she readily responds to Jesus' invitation. Martha, however, is 'too busy'.

Like me, you probably feel sorry for Martha. After all, supper was expected, and Mary, it seems, wasn't pulling her weight. When I reflect on this encounter, however, I sense that there is a Martha and a Mary in each of us. There are times when we need to be busy because life has to carry on, and there are times when we need to simply be, because it is in the quiet of the 'being' that we find the inner resources for all our 'doing'. Jesus was certainly a man of action, but he drew his strength from those quiet withdrawals to be with God in solitude and prayer.

Our inner Martha has a loud, insistent voice, forever prodding us into action. Our inner Mary sits quietly and listens. How is the balance between them? Who has the upper hand?

MARGARET SILF

Knowing the shepherd

The Lord is my shepherd, I shall not want. He makes me lie down in green pastures; he leads me beside still waters; he restores my soul. He leads me in right paths for his name's sake. Even though I walk through the darkest valley, I fear no evil; for you are with me; your rod and your staff – they comfort me. You prepare a table before me in the presence of my enemies; you anoint my head with oil; my cup overflows. Surely goodness and mercy shall follow me all the days of my life, and I shall dwell in the house of the Lord my whole life long.

Today's reading must be among the most familiar and the best-loved in all scripture. It speaks of the kind of rest and recreation that we mainly feel we can only dream of. The image of those welcoming green pastures, those soothing still waters, that all-enveloping loving presence that never abandons us even in the darkest valleys of experience – all these promises have one thing in common: they are offered to us freely by God. No amount of striving on our part will bring us to those calm waters. The Lord is the shepherd. It is he who guides us, leads us, restores us, companions us, sets a table before us and anoints us with his peace. All that is asked of us is that we lie down in his pastures and rest in him as he ministers to us.

A story is told about an overworked, over-stressed minister who organised a parish reflection day and invited a famous actor to participate, by reciting this psalm. The visitor did so with panache, and everyone applauded enthusiastically. Then the actor turned to the minister and asked him to recite the psalm in his turn. The minister was embarrassed, knowing that he could not recite the psalm with the skill of the actor. Nevertheless, he stood up and prayed the psalm. When he had finished, the parishioners were moved to tears. The actor thanked him, turned to the people and said, 'You see, my friends, I know the psalm, but your minister here, he knows the shepherd.'

The green pastures and still waters are found by those who know, and trust, the shepherd.

MARGARET SILF

Dropping the burden

'Come to me, all you that are weary and are carrying heavy burdens, and I will give you rest. Take my yoke upon you, and learn from me; for I am gentle and humble in heart, and you will find rest for your souls. For my yoke is easy, and my burden is light.'

This reading can catch us on a raw edge. It frequently doesn't feel as though our heavy burdens are relieved or that the weight of simply living from day to day is 'light'. When these feelings arise in me, I imagine a conversation with Jesus in which I tell him honestly how I am really feeling, and that the weariness won't just go away by reading this promise.

Then I imagine him inviting me, first of all, just to stop and rest for a moment. Even in the busiest schedule this should be possible. Then he invites me to put down my load, just for a while, and look at it through his eyes.

'Imagine all these burdens as parcels,' he says, 'that you are carrying on your back, day after day. Take a look at them prayerfully with me, and look at the names on them. Quite probably many of them are not even yours. It's good to help each other carry the load, but not to take responsibility for what is not your problem to solve. If you do, you may disempower someone else who will grow through the challenge it offers them.'

This reduces the pile considerably. Then Jesus goes on to ask, 'Of the parcels that remain, which of them are issues beyond your control? Don't let the things you can't change distract you from those you can.'

And so a few more parcels can be left aside. Suddenly the pile begins to look much more manageable. 'And now,' Jesus continues, 'pick up what is yours to carry, and let us carry it together. You and I are yoked together in love and compassion, and if you trust me you will discover that my yoke is not another burden but the gift that makes all burdens light.'

Spend some time with Jesus today, letting him sift through your burdens, open your eyes and offer you the gift of his yoke.

MARGARET SILF

Drawn or driven

The Lord is the everlasting God, the Creator of the ends of the earth. He does not faint or grow weary; his understanding is unsearchable. He gives power to the faint, and strengthens the powerless. Even youths will faint and be weary, and the young will fall exhausted; but those who wait for the Lord shall renew their strength, they shall mount up with wings like eagles, they shall run and not be weary, they shall walk and not faint.

Why does so much of our so-called recreation, especially in the driven climate of the western world, involve so much hyperactivity? Why do we so often feel more stressed at the end of a holiday than at the beginning? Why is our children's free time, intended for relaxation, taken over by a host of activities that can easily leave them overtired and fractious?

Today's reading invites us to do far more than organise the perfect family holiday or juggle the conflicting demands of work, home and family. It invites us to soar with the eagles. If we allow ourselves to be carried to these heights, we discover that the enterprise is wholly effortless on our part. It is fuelled entirely by the power of God, the only source of infinitely sustainable energy. It gives us strength when we are feeling drained and empowers us when we feel powerless.

Ancient wisdom warns us that 'the devil drives'. God, however, never drives. God draws. The things that drive us are like opposing winds whipping our lives into a frenzy. God's power is more like gentle thermal air streams. The birds are wiser than we are: they ride the thermals, allowing themselves to be carried to the skies by a power not their own, while we so often wrestle in vain to control the winds.

Perhaps this is the art of 'waiting for the Lord': to relax into the power that holds us in being, the first source of all we do; to let our restless striving cease; and to realise that to rest in God releases far more power and energy than any effort we can exert for ourselves.

Give yourself permission today to rest on the thermal currents
of God's love and let them raise you up.

MARGARET SILF

Let yourself be served

[Jesus] got up from the table, took off his outer robe, and tied a towel around himself. Then he poured water into a basin and began to wash the disciples' feet and to wipe them with the towel that was tied around him. He came to Simon Peter, who said to him, 'Lord, are you going to wash my feet?' Jesus answered, 'You do not know now what I am doing, but later you will understand.' Peter said to him, 'You will never wash my feet.' Jesus answered, 'Unless I wash you, you have no share with me.' Simon Peter said to him, 'Lord, not my feet only but also my hands and my head!'

This incident is packed with human detail. We can almost see Jesus wrapping the towel round his waist, rolling up his sleeves and tenderly ministering to his friends.

Imagine this scene unfolding in your own life. It's been a long, hard day. You are feeling utterly exhausted and ready to drop. Jesus knows this and, though exhausted himself, he prepares to bathe your sore feet. What might you feel? Perhaps a mix of relief and gratitude but also some embarrassment. But Jesus isn't checking whether you've done the dishes and made the beds. He's not examining your to-do list for all those unfinished jobs. He just wants to help you relax and find rest in him.

Jesus is giving his friends an example here: what he does for them, they should do for others. But this gesture of loving service is also an invitation to us to accept and enjoy the gift of rest and recovery that is being offered. The hymn 'The Servant Song' celebrates the ministry of loving service and the friend who is Christ for you, there for you in your joy and your sorrow, asking no more of you than that you receive the gift of loving care.

It isn't easy to accept such undeserved love. Perhaps the most crucial line in the hymn is the prayer for the grace to let others be as a servant to us. To rest in God's love is to let yourself receive this gift of undeserved love.

Peter at first resists Jesus' invitation to rest in this love.
How will you respond?

MARGARET SILF

Deeper than restlessness

Blessed are those who trust in the Lord, whose trust is the Lord. They shall be like a tree planted by water, sending out its roots by the stream. It shall not fear when heat comes, and its leaves shall stay green; in the year of drought it is not anxious, and it does not cease to bear fruit.

I've often heard the proverb 'Grow where you're planted', and like many others perhaps I have found it difficult to put into practice. It seems there is an almost incurable restlessness in human beings that means we are always either straining into the future or hankering for the past, imagining how life would be in some other place or circumstances or fretfully anticipating the next move.

Trees don't do that. Trees quite spectacularly embody the wisdom of resting and growing exactly where they are. Today's reading invites us to reflect on the fruits of following their example. All that is asked of us is that we put down roots beside the stream of life itself. Nothing more than this. Then our leaves will stay green and our lives will bear fruit. We will be freed of the fear of our resources drying up, because what we need will be supplied to us not through our efforts but through God's grace.

What price would we pay for a cure for our anxiety and stress, our regrets for the past and our fears for the future? What if the cure is right there in our own hearts, the roots of our being? And the prescription is simply to rest in the ground of our being and let our hearts reach down to the source of all peace?

Augustine reminds us that 'our hearts are restless until they rest in you'. When I gaze at a tree, I begin to understand the truth of these words. The branches of my life may be blown in all directions, but the roots remain, unshaken and unshakeable. Today we are invited to connect in prayer to these deep roots and simply rest in that place of peace, leaving all else to God.

Take time today to connect with your heart's deepest roots,
and let them lead you to the unending stream of God's love.

MARGARET SILF

Through rest comes re-creation

On the third day there was a wedding in Cana of Galilee, and the mother of Jesus was there. Jesus and his disciples had also been invited to the wedding. When the wine gave out, the mother of Jesus said to him, 'They have no wine'… Jesus said to them, 'Fill the jars with water.' And they filled them up to the brim. He said to them, 'Now draw some out, and take it to the chief steward.' So they took it. When the steward tasted the water that had become wine, and did not know where it came from (though the servants who had drawn the water knew), the steward called the bridegroom and said to him, 'Everyone serves the good wine first, and then the inferior wine after the guests have become drunk. But you have kept the good wine until now.'

Today we meet Jesus relaxing with his friends at the wedding of a local couple in Cana. It must have been quite a party, because we learn that the wine had already run out. Of course, this incident is primarily about the miracle of transformation, but the first lesson it offers us is this: it's okay to party! It's good to celebrate together and have a good time. In fact, it is more than good, it is blessed, and God is right in there among us as we relax and enjoy ourselves. For many of us, this realisation in itself is something of a miracle.

Jesus appears at first reluctant to be pulled out of the party mood when his mother tells him about the wine crisis. Yet he responds to her request, and at this point the account of the wedding at Cana moves beyond simple enjoyment into the realm of transformation. It moves beyond 'rest' to 're-creation', reminding us that it is in our ability and willingness to rest that we will experience re-creation, just as our bodies and minds are re-created during sleep and the water is transformed into wine during a party.

Early schooldays often began with the hymn 'Morning has broken', by Eleanor Farjeon, as we chirped our joy at 'God's re-creation of the new day'. May that simple joy continue to be re-created in us every morning.

MARGARET SILF

The still centre

On that day, when evening had come, [Jesus] said to them, 'Let us go across to the other side.' And leaving the crowd behind, they took him with them in the boat, just as he was. Other boats were with him. A great gale arose, and the waves beat into the boat, so that the boat was already being swamped. But he was in the stern, asleep on the cushion; and they woke him up and said to him, 'Teacher, do you not care that we are perishing?' He woke up and rebuked the wind, and said to the sea, 'Peace! Be still!' Then the wind ceased, and there was a dead calm. He said to them, 'Why are you afraid? Have you still no faith?' And they were filled with great awe and said to one another, 'Who then is this, that even the wind and the sea obey him?'

I once had the unhappy experience of being with a group of otherwise very friendly and peaceable people, when one of them flew into a frenzied rage, hurling irrational verbal abuse at some of those present. The effect was dramatic. Some tried to reason with the person concerned. Some left the room to escape from the raw emotion of unbridled anger. One person was unable to move and sat in his seat trembling with fear.

One single person among us, however, stayed in the circle in silent meditation. Her presence was quite remarkable. She didn't try to fix anything, but neither did she run away from it. She simply sat there in perfect stillness, and it was quite clear that she was connecting to the peace of God deep in her own heart. In doing so she held the whole situation in a place deeper than all the shouting.

Perhaps it was a bit like this during the gale described in today's reading. The storm is raging all around, and the disciples are running round in circles, helpless and filled with fear. Only one person holds the stillness. Jesus sleeps. He holds the whole situation in a place where no winds blow.

When the gales blow through our lives, may we have the grace to rest in that deeper place where God holds the still centre.

MARGARET SILF

What if?

[Jesus] said to his disciples, 'Therefore I tell you, do not worry about your life, what you will eat, or about your body, what you will wear. For life is more than food, and the body more than clothing. Consider the ravens: they neither sow nor reap, they have neither storehouse nor barn, and yet God feeds them. Of how much more value are you than the birds! And can any of you by worrying add a single hour to your span of life? If then you are not able to do so small a thing as that, why do you worry about the rest? Consider the lilies, how they grow: they neither toil nor spin, yet I tell you, even Solomon in all his glory was not clothed like one of these.'

Worry! It's probably one of the most potent threats to our ability to rest, either physically, mentally or spiritually. It keeps us awake at night and distracted by day. It really doesn't matter how often we are advised not to worry, we continue to worry. It's a nagging force that seems to refuse to be switched off.

Our higher brain has evolved to process our experience of the past and our hopes and dreams for the future. The ravens and the lilies don't have this problem or this gift. They don't, and can't, worry. So how might we respond to Jesus' warning in today's reading?

Two little words sum up the power of worry: 'What if?' They are at once the most destructive and the most creative of words. When we are fretful, we toss them around our brains, imagining all that could go wrong. Such anxiety sucks us into a downward spiral from which it is very difficult to escape. But 'what if?' can be powerfully creative, inviting us to imagine the best we can be. An intentional change of focus can turn the worry worm into a butterfly of possibility.

Jesus invites us to change our focus from the small things we worry about to the great sweep of God's care for all creation and its promise in our lives.

'Two men look through prison bars: the one sees mud, the other stars'
(Frederick Langbridge, 1849–1922). May we rise beyond the mud and
rest beneath the stars.

MARGARET SILF

Beacons of peace

Do not worry about anything, but in everything by prayer and supplication with thanksgiving let your requests be made known to God. And the peace of God, which surpasses all understanding, will guard your hearts and your minds in Christ Jesus. Finally, beloved, whatever is true, whatever is honourable, whatever is just, whatever is pure, whatever is pleasing, whatever is commendable, if there is any excellence and if there is anything worthy of praise, think about these things. Keep on doing the things that you have learned and received and heard and seen in me, and the God of peace will be with you.

Today's reading offers us a practical course of action to lead us beyond our anxieties to the peace that passes understanding and a down-to-earth guide on rising above the worries that habitually beset us.

It's a question of focus. When we focus on what is negative, we are unconsciously drawn deeper into our own negativity. Negativity is highly contagious. We risk infecting others with it or being infected by their negativity. But positivity is equally contagious. When we focus on what is truly life-affirming, we become affirmed ourselves and more affirming of each other.

Paul gives us examples of such life-giving agents: things that ring true in our hearts, that proclaim justice and command respect, things that encourage us to be the best we can be. These beacons are all around us, if we have eyes to see and hearts to recognise them: the person who protests against injustice and is not afraid to challenge dishonest practices; the child who delights us with her simple candour; the natural world that proclaims moment by moment the presence of beauty and harmony.

Make these attitudes a life habit, Paul promises, and you will find yourself worrying less and being more deeply at peace with yourself, the world and God. Often the simple act of stepping outside will be enough to persuade you to leave your worries on the doorstep as the beauty and wonder of earth and sky eclipse your anxieties and restore your perspective and your peace.

What beacons of goodness and truth have lit your path today and led you to peace? Can you let this question become a daily reflection?

MARGARET SILF

Sleeping like a baby

O Lord, my heart is not lifted up, my eyes are not raised too high; I do not occupy myself with things too great and too marvellous for me. But I have calmed and quieted my soul, like a weaned child with its mother; my soul is like a weaned child that is with me. O Israel, hope in the Lord from this time on and forevermore.

As I began my very first silent retreat many years ago, my retreat guide gave me a prayer card with this text and suggested I use it as the core of my night prayer for the coming eight days. These words imprinted themselves on my mind and still often return to me at night as I seek the gift of sleep.

A baby is perhaps the most trusting of all human beings. He knows virtually nothing, but is content to lie in his mother's arms and trust that all he needs will be supplied. She has no anxieties about the state of the world or the pressures of work, and when she raises her eyes it isn't to grasp at matters beyond her reach, but to gaze into the eyes of the one who holds her.

A baby also knows how to live in the present moment with no anxieties about the 'if onlys' and the 'what ifs' that plague our adult lives. While we look ahead and are filled with apprehension about the mountain we may have to climb tomorrow, a child simply relishes the flowers that blossom all around her on the foothills.

The psalmist urges us to emulate this level of trust, and thereby to find this depth of peace, even if we are only able to do so for a few minutes as we fall asleep. Instead of lying restlessly fretting about things we can't change, we are invited to relax into the quiet of the night and gaze into the eyes of the one who holds us in being. As we do this we can let the balloons of anxiety float away, knowing that we are firmly grounded in the heart of God.

Let us switch off all our screens, calm our souls and let the psalmist lead us to a place of rest.

MARGARET SILF

A flourishing garden

I will be like the dew to Israel; he shall blossom like the lily, he shall strike root like the forests of Lebanon. His shoots shall spread out; his beauty shall be like the olive tree, and his fragrance like that of Lebanon. They shall again live beneath my shadow, they shall flourish as a garden; they shall blossom like the vine, their fragrance shall be like the wine of Lebanon.

When I was a little girl, I often visited an elderly aunt who had a small back garden in the suburbs of a busy industrial city. In this garden there was a plaque with these words: 'The kiss of the sun for pardon, the song of the birds for mirth, one is nearer God's heart in a garden than anywhere else on earth.' Her garden was my playground and for her, no doubt, a place where she found both rest and re-creation.

Today's reading promises that God's people shall 'flourish as a garden' and delights us with a foretaste of that garden, where each shall put down deep roots, blossom and bear fruit, like the olives and the vine, filling the earth with unique beauty and fragrance. Every garden reminds us of this promise and invites us to grow into the fullness of who we can be.

Gardens grow, in spite of our efforts or even our neglect. The surge towards life is unstoppable, and asks of us only that we provide a little care, water in due season and the removal of damaging weeds. Dew forms silently upon the earth without any effort on our part and soaks deep into the ground. The dew of the Holy Spirit forms silently upon our hearts and penetrates the ground of our being, bringing life, whether or not we are aware of it. It is pure gift, asking only that we are open to receive it.

As the earth rests through the night, the dew falls gently, giving life. When we pause and rest, the soul-nourishing dew of God falls gently on our lives. Where better than a garden to come to rest?

May we find rest and re-creation in our gardens, and be willing
to share that gift with those who have no garden.

MARGARET SILF

In the sunshine of God's smile

The Lord spoke to Moses, saying: Speak to Aaron and his sons, saying, Thus you shall bless the Israelites: You shall say to them, The Lord bless you and keep you; the Lord make his face to shine upon you, and be gracious to you; the Lord lift up his countenance upon you, and give you peace. So they shall put my name on the Israelites, and I will bless them.

There is a particular house that I pass regularly when I walk around the local lanes. Its front bay window is filled with an elaborate arrangement of cat baskets, and usually at least one cat, and often two, are in residence, basking in the sun and totally at rest. Cats are wonderful models of how to rest. It is estimated that they spend up to 16 hours a day asleep.

If cats could read, they would recognise the blessing in today's reading. They know all about letting the sun shine on them and lull them into peaceful repose. All well and good, you might say, but we are not cats, and we don't have the luxury of a cosy resting place in which to bask, let alone 16 hours for an extended daily nap.

Or perhaps we do? A friend recently shared his thoughts on how, for him, the sun is a reminder of the nature of God. The sun is silent and remote, and yet it warms every cell in our bodies. It doesn't proclaim its presence or force itself on us. It simply is what it is. It simply shines. What's more, it shines all the time, and when we think it isn't shining, it's because the clouds come between us. God, too, is who God is. For much of the time, God may seem to us to be silent and remote, and yet this source of life itself never ceases for a moment to enfold us in the arms of eternal love. Not 16 hours a day, but 24.

May the face of that love shine down upon us and fill us with God's grace. May that loving presence rise anew for us every day, like sunrise, bestowing the blessing that will never fail, whatever clouds may appear to come between us.

MARGARET SILF

The ten commandments

During this season of Lent we are challenged to look again at the ten commandments and what they might mean in our lives today. These ancient instructions are at the heart of Jewish and Christian moral teaching and have deeply influenced western legal and social thinking over the centuries. After the Reformation they gained renewed prominence in England and became a key element of the local church's teaching work. Boards with the commandments began to appear in parish churches, and in 1604 bishops were instructed to ensure that the 'ten commandments be set upon the east end of every church and chapel where the people may best see and read the same'. But by the end of the 19th century the boards had gone out of fashion and many were removed. The commandments lost their prominent place in the national consciousness.

Today many people in the UK, Christians included, would struggle to name all ten commandments, let alone number them. Many people regard them as being part of a negative religion of the past, at odds with the ethos and needs of today. Christians too have wanted to escape what feels like a 'Thou shalt not' religion, as they try to witness to the abounding love of God for all. So, ask yourself, how do you react to these ancient commands?

As we explore the commands this Lent, I hope we can discover again their place within a story of amazing community liberation and a deep encounter with the God of compassion, justice and truth. It is then that they can come alive anew and truly challenge us to be born again – to claim that freedom that God wants for us all, a freedom not at the expense of others but for the good of all.

The season of Lent invites us to reflect on ways in which we fall short of God's desire for our lives and to recognise our deep need for that compassion and forgiveness which we see shining through the life of Jesus. Some Christian traditions use the ten commandments as part of a prayer of confession during Lent. The Methodist Ash Wednesday service includes the reading of each commandment with the prayer response: 'Lord, have mercy on us and turn our hearts to delight in your law.'

TERRY HINKS

Liberating law

Israel camped there in front of the mountain. Then Moses went up to God; the Lord called to him from the mountain, saying, 'Thus you shall say to the house of Jacob, and tell the Israelites: You have seen what I did to the Egyptians, and how I bore you on eagles' wings and brought you to myself. Now therefore, if you obey my voice and keep my covenant, you shall be my treasured possession out of all the peoples. Indeed, the whole earth is mine, but you shall be for me a priestly kingdom and a holy nation.'

The ten commandments in the book of Exodus begin by reminding the people that it was God who led them out of slavery in Egypt. It is from the act of compassion and liberation that the commandments arise. That is important for Christians to note, because at times a false distinction has been made between a legalistic religion and a Spirit-led faith. The Exodus vision is not of God liberating his people with one hand and then enslaving them with rules and regulations with the other. The commandments are given to form the new liberated community, a healthy community in contrast to the death-dealing empire they have escaped.

The great Jewish thinker Martin Buber describes the commandments as part of our encounter with the living God – an I/thou relationship rather than some impersonal rule book. The encounter with God is essential to breathe life – and the Spirit – into the commands that follow.

So, as you reflect on the commandments, make space for that encounter. Picture the God who bore the people of Israel on eagles' wings and brought them to the place of encounter with the divine. Picture yourself being carried on eagles' wings, lifted beyond all that limits you; sense the excitement and exhilaration of flying high, seeing the world from above; know yourself carried by the God of all life. Know too that this is God's desire for those closest to your heart – and those farthest away. God desires to bring all closer – to touch all with grace, truth and love.

Mother God, hold your world in your loving care;
give us all new vision and new love.

TERRY HINKS

No other gods

The Lord said to [Moses], 'Go down, and come up bringing Aaron with you; but do not let either the priests or the people break through to come up to the Lord; otherwise he will break out against them.' So Moses went down to the people and told them. Then God spoke all these words: I am the Lord your God, who brought you out of the land of Egypt, out of the house of slavery; you shall have no other gods before me.

God speaks and reaches out to the people of Israel – affirming the divine nature as 'I am who I am', but also their God who brought them out of Egypt, out of slavery. The fundamentals of Israel's God are laid out so plainly in one simple sentence. The command to have no other gods arises from that nature and that relationship. It is a covenantal, committed relationship not to be jettisoned in hard or easy times, not to be watered down by mixed loyalties. God is committed to the people and is gloriously and gracefully allowing them to claim the divine as 'their God' and themselves as 'God's people'.

The unseeable God becomes personal and, in that sense, exclusive. But that brings with it dangers. It is perhaps inevitable that the first command has been seen in tribal terms – our god in opposition to your god. While people live in their own religious bubbles, that approach is reasonably unproblematic. However, once people are brought into close proximity with people of other faiths, the 'tribal god' can either cause terrible strife or deep-rooted confusion.

A 2017 YouGov survey found that the majority of people in the UK agreed with the last six commandments, but few felt that the first four, relating to God, were relevant today. People were particularly dismissive of the first commandment – not to have any other gods. They perhaps felt that the nation was now a place of many faiths and no single faith should be allowed a monopoly over truth. Tribal gods will not suffice, yet ultimately, in whatever way God is proclaimed and worshipped, is there not one God alone?

One God, beyond all our labels, to you be glory given this day.

TERRY HINKS

Images and idols

You shall not make for yourself an idol, whether in the form of anything that is in heaven above, or that is on the earth beneath, or that is in the water under the earth. You shall not bow down to them or worship them; for I the Lord your God am a jealous God, punishing children for the iniquity of parents, to the third and the fourth generation of those who reject me, but showing steadfast love to the thousandth generation of those who love me and keep my commandments.

What is an idol for you? What are the images that have power over you? Alongside the coronavirus pandemic and the American elections, 2020 will be remembered for the Black Lives Matter protests. One key moment in the UK was when the statue of the slave trader Edward Coulson was pulled down in Bristol and dragged to the river. For some, the focus on statuary was a distraction from the graver issues of the injustices, prejudice and oppression black people face; for others, it was an important element of the struggle for true recognition. Images do carry power in society and in the living out of faith in the divine.

In fact, in today's technological society, we are bombarded with images – on phone, TV screen and computer. Those images take many forms and are often positive and life-affirming. Yet they are also powerful and at times these created images, be they virtual, verbal or actual, can be immensely damaging – to the one portrayed or the one looking.

God is beyond our imagination or description, and our approach to any image must keep that in mind. The command to avoid creating any idols is an outworking of the first command to have no other gods – to offer worship only to God. Yet there is a distinct challenge in this command. We may construct images and icons out of the best of motives, but there is always the danger that, far from being a window into God (or God's creation), they become a barrier to or distortion of the God who cannot be contained.

Reflect on the images you see today – and know the God
who is beyond all images, beyond our imagination.

TERRY HINKS

Keeping God at the centre

You shall not make wrongful use of the name of the Lord your God, for the Lord will not acquit anyone who misuses his name. Remember the sabbath day, and keep it holy. For six days you shall labour and do all your work. But the seventh day is a sabbath to the Lord your God; you shall not do any work – you, your son or your daughter, your male or female slave, your livestock, or the alien resident in your towns. For in six days the Lord made heaven and earth, the sea, and all that is in them, but rested the seventh day; therefore the Lord blessed the sabbath day and consecrated it.

God is at the centre in the first two commandments, above all other gods or idols, and the second two commandments keep that focus, challenging the people of Israel not to misuse God's name, creation or time. Above all, the name and nature of God is at the heart of today's passage, and I invite you to reflect on the God described here and God in your own life.

The word translated here as 'Lord' is the sacred name, YHWH, so holy that Jewish tradition holds that it should not be spoken. It is the extra-ordinary 'I am who I am' name that Moses was given in his encounter with the divine through the burning bush. God is not one being among many; God is God, the ground of all being. Yet remarkably this source of being is the people's God – a God in relationship with humanity, and not just humanity but all life. God is the maker, the creator of heaven and earth, the sea and all that is in them – creatures in all their myriad forms. Alongside all this, God is the maker of time itself, the rhythm of activity and rest. Finally, God is the God who blesses, makes holy and transforms reality with grace.

That is the name and nature of God, and such a God is worthy of our worship, our time and our respect. God is not a name to bandy about care-lessly, as we will explore further tomorrow.

God of one nature and many names, accept our worship today.

TERRY HINKS

The holy name

Thus you shall keep my commandments and observe them: I am the Lord. You shall not profane my holy name, that I may be sanctified among the people of Israel: I am the Lord; I sanctify you, I who brought you out of the land of Egypt to be your God: I am the Lord.

Apple, Amazon, Facebook, Google and Microsoft – how do you react to the names of these tech giants? Gratefully or suspiciously? Our lives today are surrounded by big names and famous brands in the worlds of industry, commerce, sport and entertainment. Yet these names can be sullied by scandal. The largest motor manufacturer in the world, Volkswagen, had built up an impressive reputation over the years since World War II, but in 2015 was exposed in the so-called Dieselgate or emissions scandal. Volkswagen was found to have deliberately programmed its diesel engines to supress emissions during laboratory testing, to meet stringent US and other national standards. Rebuilding the company's reputation has cost millions.

Names are important in human relationships, bound up as they are with identity and story. The liberation of the people of Israel in the story of the exodus had in a sense begun with the revealing of God's name. In his encounter with the divine through the burning bush Moses is given the Lord's innermost name – I am who I am. God is the God of Abraham and their ancestors, but more than that God is God, the very being of being.

Revealing that name is an act of utter grace – and one that Moses and the people recognise as an immense privilege. Such a name is not to be used lightly. No wonder they chose not to speak the name aloud in honour of its holy quality. Yet they carried the name, and the challenge was not to profane it, not simply by speaking it carelessly but by actions at odds with God's ways. Sadly, all too easily people of faith can be glib or hypocritical when they speak of God and speak to God. May the holy name inspire us to better things.

Lord Jesus, guard us from saying 'Lord, Lord'
and failing to do your will. Amen

TERRY HINKS

The holy day

[Jesus] said to them, 'The sabbath was made for humankind, and not humankind for the sabbath; so the Son of Man is lord even of the sabbath.' Again he entered the synagogue, and a man was there who had a withered hand. They watched him to see whether he would cure him on the sabbath, so that they might accuse him. And he said to the man who had the withered hand, 'Come forward.' Then he said to them, 'Is it lawful to do good or to do harm on the sabbath, to save life or to kill?' But they were silent.

The fourth commandment flows from the first three: the sabbath day is to be holy, set aside to reflect the rhythm of creation and the creator. No longer slaves and obliged to work at their owners' whim, they can rest as God rested in creation. The sabbath day is blessed and a blessing, yet from early days there was debate as to who and what should be included.

At the time of Jesus, the debate within Judaism was fierce and it was over the keeping of this commandment that Jesus received the most criticism, being often accused of breaking the sabbath regulations. Jesus enters the debate on the side of mercy and humanity, rather than strict regulation keeping. To do good, such as rescuing an animal or healing a man, is in Jesus' eyes lawful. The sabbath rest was made, he argues, for humanity, for the benefit of our souls and minds, but that does not mean the sustaining and saving work of God and his Christ should cease on that day.

What about us today in our modern 24/7 society? During the 2020–21 pandemic, lockdowns brought enforced rest on some and extra work and pressures on others. Doing good in health and care work (and supplying the nation with food) cannot be left to six out of seven days. But the people who provide this work need time and space to rest too. We all need to create healthy rhythms of purposeful activity and restful recreation and ensure that others can do so too.

---

*Pause – for your own good, for the good of others,
for the good of the planet.*

TERRY HINKS

Right relationships

Honour your father and your mother, so that your days may be long in the land that the Lord your God is giving you. You shall not murder. You shall not commit adultery. You shall not steal. You shall not bear false witness against your neighbour.

After the focus on God, holy and eternal, the commands shift to the human relationships within the new liberated community. While the final five commands are written in negative terms, the first is couched positively with a promise attached, inviting the hearers to honour their parents, that their days may be long. This is not about unquestioning worship or blind obedience; God alone is worthy of worship.

Jesus had challenging moments in relation to his family, resisting their demand that he return home and keep out of trouble (Mark 3:21, 31–35). He challenged the commandment in three ways: heightening the worth of the child – 'it is to such as these that the kingdom of heaven belongs' (Matthew 19:14); recognising that faith can at times divide families rather than unite them; and redefining family by pointing to his disciples and saying, 'Whoever does the will of God is my mother.' Still, Jesus no doubt honoured his parents, both in the early years of his childhood and to the very end of his life. At the cross Jesus places his mother in the care of a beloved disciple, and vice versa (John 19:26–27). This is a true honouring of a woman who was experiencing the deepest of pains – the death of her child.

In all this Jesus shows that the command needs both to be taken to heart and to be interpreted with care and kindness. Family relationships are complicated and ever have been. Parents mess up; children do likewise. Sometimes the failures by parents are deeper and more terrible – abuse, neglect, even murder. The 'honour' killings which still take place today are perhaps the most terrible reversal of the true nature of the command.

Even in the most well-adjusted of families, expectations between parents and children can be heavy on both sides, yet at its best the relationship of child to parent can give us an insight into the very nature of God's love for us.

Thank God for each child born this day, praying that they may know love.

TERRY HINKS

Stop the killing

Cain said to his brother Abel, 'Let us go out to the field.' And when they were in the field, Cain rose up against his brother Abel and killed him. Then the Lord said to Cain, 'Where is your brother Abel?' He said, 'I do not know; am I my brother's keeper?' And the Lord said, 'What have you done? Listen; your brother's blood is crying out to me from the ground!'

Killing has a long history among humans, first with the killing of animals for food and then the killing of rivals in the hunt for that food or to protect territory claimed. It reached new levels of horror and efficiency in the 20th century with the attempted extermination of whole races in holocaust and genocide, in the threat to all life in the nuclear arms race and the policy of mutually assured destruction. While we have been spared another world war, violence remains widespread in our world today. Its portrayal is part of our daily entertainment in film, TV and video games. When will the killing stop?

The first murder in the Bible story is a grim affair, the result of mounting tension between brothers and the bitter resentment felt by the less favoured one. Questioned by God, Cain denies knowledge of his brother's fate, with words that have entered our vocabulary, 'Am I my brother's keeper?' Cain may deny it – to God and perhaps even to himself – but God confronts him with reality. Listen to the ground, God says, listen to the earth. The blood of your brother is crying out.

When will humanity learn a better way? The debate continues as to how far the command 'You shall not kill' extends. Is it about murder, or killing more generally? What is being prohibited or allowed? The Exodus story, after all, has its fair share of killing. Yet ultimately it is best to read the command at its simplest and to reflect on how all life is precious and ultimately belongs to God. We tread on sacred ground that cries out against human violence.

Reflect on the words of Christ, whose gift is peace: 'Blessed are the peacemakers, for they will be called children of God' (Matthew 5:9).

TERRY HINKS

Faithful relationships

'You have heard that it was said, "You shall not commit adultery." But I say to you that everyone who looks at a woman with lust has already committed adultery with her in his heart. If your right eye causes you to sin, tear it out and throw it away; it is better for you to lose one of your members than for your whole body to be thrown into hell.'

What have you heard about recently in the area of human relationships and sexuality? The #MeToo movement and sexual harassment in the workplace? Gay marriage and the church's attitude to homosexuality? Questions of gender identity and transgender people? Divorce and remarriage? A veritable storm of issues confronts us today, as human beings learn again how to build good relationships and the place of sexuality within them. The command 'You shall not commit adultery' might not connect with all these issues, but it does remind us that faithfulness and integrity are critical to deep and healthy relationships. Unlike most societies in the ancient Near East, Israel regarded adultery as contrary to God's intention for human relationships. It was seen as an act of disloyalty that undermined the integrity of the marriage covenant.

Far from abandoning the law, Jesus challenges his disciples to go further and deeper in their living out of God's commands. So, in a fashion typical of Jewish rabbis of the time, he speaks in exaggerated terms of tearing out an eye if it gets in the way of God's desire for our lives. He interprets adultery in terms of attitude rather than simply a physical sexual act.

In this he takes us closer to the heart of the command, which is far less about sex than we tend to assume and far more about faithfulness and commitment. That focus on faithfulness and integrity in human relationships, both by the people of Israel and by Jesus, reflected their belief in the faithful love of their God. God is not fickle or changing in his compassion towards us; can we reflect that in our relationships today?

'Give thanks to the Lord, because he is good.
His faithful love continues forever' (Psalm 107:1, NIRV).

TERRY HINKS

Stolen lives

You shall not steal; you shall not deal falsely; and you shall not lie to one another. And you shall not swear falsely by my name, profaning the name of your God: I am the Lord. You shall not defraud your neighbour; you shall not steal; and you shall not keep for yourself the wages of a labourer until morning.

As an enslaved people in Egypt, the Israelites had their rights and freedoms stolen from them. From being property owners, they had in effect become the property of others. In their new-found, God-given freedom, they could be their own people with their own belongings. Respecting each other's belongings was part of living out that new freedom and that new sense of common purpose. Stealing, dishonesty and fraud were at odds with all they had won, and such acts risked breaking that sense of mutual care on which they relied.

Perhaps you – or someone close to you – have experienced theft in one way or another. It may have been a break-in at your property, the stealing of your car, a mugging, a scam or fraud, or identity theft. To be a victim of such crime brings a whole raft of destructive emotions. It can feel like a violation not just of your things, but of you.

Yet, as today's reading reminds us, theft extends beyond these legal crimes. The book of Leviticus links stealing with defrauding neighbours and withholding wages. Prophets such as Isaiah and Amos took up this message in their attacks on the injustices and corrupt practices they saw in society.

Today our increasingly unequal society has allowed some to become extraordinarily rich on the backs of many who are desperately poor and who have been effectively robbed of a fair wage. We have all benefited from goods produced cheaply, but all too often under appalling conditions, in unfair systems and at great harm to the environment. We need to ask in every purchase we make: are we stealing from others in the things we buy? Are we robbing the natural world, the planet itself, to provide ourselves the comforts we take for granted?

Look out for Fairtrade products today and learn more about its campaigns.
Reflect on the stories behind the products you buy.

TERRY HINKS

Trustworthy?

There are six things that the Lord hates, seven that are an abomination to him: haughty eyes, a lying tongue, and hands that shed innocent blood, a heart that devises wicked plans, feet that hurry to run to evil, a lying witness who testifies falsely, and one who sows discord in a family.

Today's reading from the book of Proverbs echoes the ninth commandment not to bear false witness (it's worth noting that different Christian traditions number the commands slightly differently). Amid the seven sins listed in the passage, lying and false testimony are both listed as an abomination to God – a typically Jewish poetic repetition to underscore their importance.

Faithfulness and honesty run through the commandments. Without them relationships become strained and fraught. In recent years western society has been battered by fake news, spin, unsubstantiated opinion, conspiracy theories, manipulative advertising, deep-running prejudice and bare-faced lies. Social media and the internet have become breeding grounds for 'lying tongues'. We have seen this disease infect our industrial, commercial and political life, resulting in a deep cynicism among many people. Without that honesty trust breaks down and society starts to seize up.

Agatha Christie's detective Miss Marple appears as a gentle old lady, but she has a sharp mind and a deep desire for justice. There is a point in one story where a character asks why they hadn't realised who the murderer was. Miss Marple replies, 'Because you believed what he told you. It's very dangerous to believe people – I haven't for years.'

In a UK survey, politicians, journalists and estate agents came out as the least trusted professionals. Doctors, judges, teachers and scientists were the most trusted. Levels of trust in church ministers have fallen in recent years and, though they remain one of the more trusted professionals, they were recently pipped by hairdressers. Scandals and accusations of hypocrisy have undermined trust in the church too. That trust will take years of hard and humble work to rebuild, but it is work that must be done – in church and society – for the good of all.

Pray for a renewing of honesty and integrity within every part
of the life of our society.

TERRY HINKS

Heart matters

You shall not covet your neighbour's house; you shall not covet your neighbour's wife, or male or female slave, or ox, or donkey, or anything that belongs to your neighbour. When all the people witnessed the thunder and lightning, the sound of the trumpet, and the mountain smoking, they were afraid and trembled and stood at a distance, and said to Moses, 'You speak to us, and we will listen; but do not let God speak to us, or we will die.' Moses said to the people, 'Do not be afraid; for God has come only to test you and to put the fear of him upon you so that you do not sin.'

We come today to the final command – 'You shall not covet.' It reminds us that we are not dealing with law and legislation but matters of heart and mind. This is not a rule that can be policed or upheld in the courtroom. It is a direction of the heart, and only God can see into the reaches of our hearts. The famous 'collect of purity' is what we need here, a prayer that begins with the words, 'Almighty God, to whom all hearts are open, all desires known, and from whom no secrets are hidden, cleanse the thoughts of our hearts by the inspiration of your Holy Spirit' (Book of Common Prayer, 1662).

Our attitudes are influenced by the society of which we are part. Ours is in many ways an affluent, greedy and addictive society. We are encouraged by advertising, media and peer pressure to want more, to constantly update our devices, to turn 'wants' into 'needs', 'luxuries' into 'essentials'. We may not want the coat from our neighbour's back, but we would like one just as good or that much better; after all, 'we're worth it'. We are left discontented with what we have or who we are. The human appetite appears to be insatiable, and the effect on our planet and on our poorer neighbours is catastrophic.

So, come back to the God who sees into your heart, better than you can yourself. Do not be afraid, but allow that divine grace to test what you most desire and renew your heart and mind in love.

'Search me, O God, and know my heart' (Psalm 139:23).

TERRY HINKS

Love and law

Owe no one anything, except to love one another; for the one who loves another has fulfilled the law. The commandments, 'You shall not commit adultery; You shall not murder; You shall not steal; You shall not covet'; and any other commandment, are summed up in this word, 'Love your neighbour as yourself.' Love does no wrong to a neighbour; therefore, love is the fulfilling of the law.

How, then, would you sum up the commandments we have been reflecting on? Have they challenged and inspired you, or felt strange and distant to you? Have they been liberating or stifling? When people look at Paul's attitude to the law, they sometimes presume that it was a negative one. They assume that he counted the law as part of the rubbish he rejected in order to gain Christ. However, in reality, Paul honoured the law as one of the great gifts of God, while recognising that none of us fully live up to its requirements. 'All have sinned and fall short of the glory of God,' he writes (Romans 3:23), and all rely on the grace of God for redemption – grace shown in Christ Jesus.

When Paul then considers the Christian response to that grace in the later chapters of his letter to the Romans, his key word is 'love', reflecting the love of God in Christ Jesus. He looks again at the commandments through this lens of love. Listing four from the commandments – those that focus on our relationship to each other in society – he adds the cover-all 'any other commandment'. Then, influenced one feels by Jesus himself, he writes that they are all summed up and fulfilled by the command, 'Love your neighbour as yourself.' Here is part of the great commandment Jesus gave, in his answer to the scribe, drawn from Leviticus 19:18 and combined so brilliantly with the command to love God with heart, soul, strength and mind.

Love is the word we must carry as we live out the ten commandments in our own context today.

Who is my neighbour? The person next door? The people who think like me? Or humanity in all its strange and glorious diversity? And the creatures and life forms that share this planet with me?

TERRY HINKS

What more must I do?

A man ran up and knelt before [Jesus], and asked him, 'Good Teacher, what must I do to inherit eternal life?' Jesus said to him, 'Why do you call me good? No one is good but God alone. You know the commandments: "You shall not murder; You shall not commit adultery; You shall not steal; You shall not bear false witness; You shall not defraud; Honour your father and mother."' He said to him, 'Teacher, I have kept all these since my youth.' Jesus, looking at him, loved him and said, 'You lack one thing; go, sell what you own, and give the money to the poor, and you will have treasure in heaven; then come, follow me.'

In a story repeated in Matthew and Luke's gospels, a man asks what he must do to inherit eternal life. Jesus first reminds the man of the utter goodness of God – only God is truly good. Then in answer to the question, he points the man to the commandments, or at least those relating to relationships with other people. They are quoted in a slightly different order to those in Exodus (and vary in the different gospel accounts), but there is no doubt of the importance that Jesus is attaching to them. They are part of the life in abundance, the eternal life, that Jesus came to share.

The man immediately replies that he has kept these commands since his youth. For him, the religious tick list is complete. This is the rub. If we treat the commandments as a set of tasks to complete, we mistake what they are really about. The commands, we have discovered, describe the essentials of a healthy relationship to the living God and to one another. In that, they are important for Jesus and for us. But Jesus calls us to do more – to let go of the things that hold us back in following him and to reach out in compassion to people weighed down by poverty or need. Just as God brought the Israelites out of slavery, Jesus desires to liberate us today. Will we allow the commandments to lead us forward into following Christ now and sharing in the work of God's kingdom?

Lead me on, Lord. Help me to follow you today.

TERRY HINKS

Remembering Holy Week and Easter

 We all remember Easter 2020 – how could we forget? We had recently entered lockdown: churches, shops, restaurants and sports facilities were closed and most people were confined at home. Those who weren't were sick or dying, or ministering to them, or providing vital key services. And that was still the case in Easter 2021. Easter is a time for remembering the death and resurrection of Jesus. For the past two years, most people have had a novel, unique and perhaps not entirely joyful experience of Holy Week and Easter. Those memories will endure.

It is not our task this year to look back on previous ones. Nevertheless, memories colour this year with new hues of both sadness and joy as we walk the way of the cross with Jesus to the Easter dawn and beyond. This year we must also re-member it. As members of the body of Christ, we are the church: the membership of Christ. We were dismembered by the coronavirus; this year we hope to re-member ourselves as Christ's church body, in fellowship, praise and thanksgiving.

Over the past two years, we have learnt about social distancing outside the closed doors of the church. Through service, care and prayer, we learnt to care for others in new ways. In 2020 the Archbishop of Canterbury celebrated Easter Day from his Lambeth kitchen: a new kind of Easter that helped many churches renew and re-create themselves online.

So this year a reconstructed church reconvenes and remembers Christ's passion and resurrection, providing on another scale a delayed resurrection to the suffering and grief of the past two Aprils. In April 2020 and 2021, we lived a long Good Friday. This year we rejoice in renewal, re-membership and resurrection hope.

First, however, we must walk that bewildering journey through suffering and death: the way of the cross. We recall some moments of Jesus' journey, to illuminate our own. Palm Sunday to Easter week is a journey from darkness to light, and this year this is a reality too poignant for those who have been buffeted and bruised by grief, confusion or mental torment. We will survey the late-Lenten landscape with new eyes this year, and walk in Christ's way with new wonder, new sorrow, new hope, new light.

GORDON GILES

Palm Sunday

'Go into the village ahead of you, and as you enter it you will find tied there a colt that has never been ridden. Untie it and bring it here. If anyone asks you, "Why are you untying it?" just say this: "The Lord needs it."'

On Palm Sunday Jesus was at the height of his popularity, the celebrity whom crowds flocked to see. Yet planning was needed. Now as then, on an important occasion detail needs to be attended to. Guest speakers need meeting at the station or a parking space reserved. Someone must book a taxi for newly-weds to leave the reception. The best-laid plans have to be laid well, otherwise inconvenience, embarrassment and even humiliation can follow and the event gets remembered for all the wrong reasons.

Has that ever happened to you? Has a big event gone wrong because you – or someone else – forgot to do something essential? Or sometimes it is just bad luck. Often we hear of a bride travelling in a classic car that failed to start, conked out or just limped to the wedding, delaying everything. Skilled organisers generally do not overlook things, but even if they do, they are good at adapting. This is why people employ wedding planners and undertakers. Over the past two years, many weddings had to be cancelled, postponed or altered because of the coronavirus. Meanwhile undertakers were busy.

Palm Sunday was more like a wedding than a funeral. Planning paid off. Even the crowd played their part (but got the message wrong). Jesus arrived like a Roman victor, yet riding on a humble beast of burden. The lamb of God arrived on a donkey. As we begin Holy Week, we remember that Jesus needed a donkey to reveal the humility of his glory before becoming the lamb of God to take away the sins of the world. For the glory of God is not the glory of anyone else, and is unlike any glory with which the crowd might have been familiar. It is a unique, servant–king glory that glows with integrity, vulnerability and service. It needs no raised palms, other than those of Jesus himself, ready to submit to piercing by bitter nails.

How can you plan your Holy Week to glorify God?

GORDON GILES

Holy Monday

'A man carrying a jar of water will meet you; follow him into the house he enters and say to the owner of the house, "The teacher asks you, 'Where is the guest room, where I may eat the Passover with my disciples?'" He will show you a large room upstairs, already furnished. Make preparations for us there.'

Yesterday we remembered how Jesus sent his disciples to get a colt. A few days later he planned and delegated again, sending them to book an upstairs room for the Passover. This time, the lamb of God will not be on a donkey, but on a plate. In a recasting of the Passover meal, Jesus took the bread and wine, and said, 'This is me. Keep doing this to remember me.' The Passover recalls the Israelites' exodus flight from the Egyptians across the sea (Exodus 12—14). Jesus, as New Testament Passover lamb, invites us to remember himself as the pioneer of a new journey (a second exodus) of faith and salvation.

Often we only focus on the key players in a drama. The last supper is about Jesus, the bread and wine and Judas leaving early to go and betray Jesus. But there are other characters backstage, or barely noticed. Who cooked the meal? Who was the man with the jar of water? He is not the owner, so who is? Was he or the owner of the room a secret disciple? Did they have any idea what a significant event they were about to quietly host? These were people whose calling was to serve the servant king, the lamb of God who the following day would be offering himself on the Passover plate of the cross.

We all need to be like that man with the water jar who is told to prepare a room. We also need to prepare room in our hearts to welcome Jesus as Holy Week continues. As we remember the events in order, we may feel spiritually remote, distanced socially from this ancient event in the past. Yet we are not mere observers, because we are invited to remember and re-member Christ in our own bodies, by sharing in his ongoing, eternal supper of faith and love.

How can you make room for Jesus this Easter?

GORDON GILES

Holy Tuesday

Then he took a loaf of bread, and when he had given thanks, he broke it and gave it to them, saying, 'This is my body, which is given for you. Do this in remembrance of me.' And he did the same with the cup after supper, saying, 'This cup that is poured out for you is the new covenant in my blood.'

The French author Marcel Proust wrote a series of novels called *In Search of Lost Time* ('À la recherche du temps perdu'). Its key theme is involuntary memory: the way in which things resurface in our minds unexpectedly. The most famous moment in the books, relished by philosophers and psychologists alike, is the moment when the narrator dips a madeleine into his tea. He shudders and his senses are invaded by a pleasurable memory of his childhood when he used to eat such cakes, and the full memory of people, places and youthful delight comes flooding back, beyond his conscious control. Such experiences happen to us all, when a personal association invades our thoughts and emotions, joyously, painfully, poignantly. Objects, flavours, sensations, even turns of phrase, can do this to us.

We can also give objects such associations. We buy souvenirs of holidays, give and receive presents. Many of us possess objects which remind us of the people who gave them, who may have passed away. In this, whether voluntarily or not, there is, at least for us, something of them in that object. Memories can be reignited this way, sometimes unpredictably when we are caught unawares by these personal associations.

For many months in 2020–21, it was not possible to receive Holy Communion. Churches were closed and, at Easter and beyond, the sharing of bread and wine was impractical for health reasons. There was much debate about this. As summer progressed, Communion returned, only the bread, no wine. It may be even as you read this that you have not tasted Holy Communion for a very long time. Even I, a priest, did not for four months. When I did, it was a Proustian moment, as more than the taste of bread and wine came to me. Perhaps it was or will be for you.

Can you taste and see how gracious the Lord is?

GORDON GILES

Holy Wednesday

[Peter] said to him, 'Lord, I am ready to go with you to prison and to death!' Jesus said, 'I tell you, Peter, the cock will not crow this day, until you have denied three times that you know me.'

Sometimes other people say things that we know we are going to remember as soon as they are said. Words of love, commitment, cruelty or pain cannot be unsaid. Words of love that are rejected or welcomed, proposals of marriage, harsh words of condemnation (fair or unjust) and the phone call or knock at the door to break the news of a death become memorable instantly. They are seared into our souls indelibly. I know exactly where I was and what I was doing when my mother rang me to say my brother had died. One does not have to 'remember' these things; they never descend to the depths of what the Greeks called 'the river of forgetfulness' (Lethe), but remain ever present and, alongside deep regret, remain fresh.

It is from the river of forgetfulness that we get the concept of truth. The Greek word is *alethea*: that which passes not into the river of forgetfulness. Things that are true are memorable. This is why some predictions affect us like the emotionally charged remembrances of love, hate, joy and pain. Jesus' prediction to Peter, 'You will deny me three times', is memorable, searing and true. Yet Peter forgot.

This is striking. If someone predicted something so significant to you, how could you forget? There are two possible answers that may help us understand Peter as being so like you and me. First, perhaps Peter wasn't listening. I do not mean he did not hear, but perhaps he was not listening. This seems unlikely, because he objects. He heard what Jesus said all right, and Jesus was telling the truth. Second, this truthful analysis of Peter's character – 'You are the kind of person who would deny me' – was so accurate that instead of remembering it in order to prevent it from happening, he suppressed it so well that a few hours later he had forgotten. Like a hypnotist's spell, or a childhood biscuit, only the cockcrow released the soul-destroying memory.

What have you forgotten about faith that you really must remember?

GORDON GILES

Maundy Thursday

Peter said, 'Man, I do not know what you are talking about!' At that moment, while he was still speaking, the cock crowed. The Lord turned and looked at Peter. Then Peter remembered the word of the Lord, how he had said to him, 'Before the cock crows today, you will deny me three times.' And he went out and wept bitterly.

Gallicantu is the Latin onomatopoeic word for the screech of the cock-crow. Since 457AD a church of St Peter in Gallicantu has stood overlooking Jerusalem, and 'holy steps' descend to the city below. Many have walked on the stones, now unstable, which Jesus trod for his night-time trial and incarceration after the last supper. Pilgrimage is about a sense of place, and one way to remember and re-member Jesus as a real presence on earth is to stand where he stood and walk where he walked.

The night scene of the courtyard of Peter's denial is one of the dark moments of Holy Week. Human weakness is revealed in that common phenomenon: letting oneself down. Peter let Jesus down, but in one sense he was already forgiven for that. Jesus knew his character and so could predict and even plan for his denial. This is no consolation for Peter, because he has let himself down as well as others, and even though Jesus forgave him on the Galilee beach after the resurrection, Peter had to live with his actions and struggled to fully accept his forgiveness and to forgive himself. Tradition has it that this is why he asked to be crucified upside down.

Salvation is not about 'forgiving ourselves'. Perhaps you are one of many who live with the guilt of something that still lives within you, a dark screech that resounds in your guts, a daily remembrance of regret or burden of self-loathing. 'I hate myself for…' is not such a rare phrase. Release is possible through the saving death and resurrection of Jesus Christ, who has stood in our punishment place on the cross to take our guilt away. And one of the things this enables, for those who can recognise it, is the ability not only to be forgiven by a higher power, but also to forgive oneself.

Ask God to help you forgive yourself.

GORDON GILES

Good Friday

'We indeed have been condemned justly, for we are getting what we deserve for our deeds, but this man has done nothing wrong.' Then he said, 'Jesus, remember me when you come into your kingdom.' He replied, 'Truly I tell you, today you will be with me in Paradise.'

I took a parish group to the underground cistern beneath Caiaphas' house in Jerusalem and after reading about Jesus' arrest in Gethsemane we sang the Taizé chant: 'Jesus, remember me, when you come into your kingdom.' Brother Roger of Taizé deserves praise and thanksgiving for the mellifluous meditative chant that so many know and love, the text of which comes from the penitent thief. That Brother Roger himself was to meet a brutal end during an evening prayer service in August 2005 adds a poignancy to that petition of hope from a man whose time was up. Like so many who die suddenly, when he entered the church to say his prayers, Brother Roger had no inkling that he was entering his final minutes.

That pit beneath the church is supposedly where Jesus was imprisoned on the night before his crucifixion, traditionally associated not only with the illegal trial before the high priest Caiaphas, but also with the courtyard in which the cock crowed as Peter denied Jesus. Unlike Brother Roger, and those thieves, Jesus knew his remaining hours were numbered. A criminal lives under the constant threat of capture and punishment, but harbours the hope of evasion. The three men on their crosses had very different journeys, expectations and attitudes to their own impending deaths.

The coronavirus has focused our minds on our own mortality, perhaps exceptionally so. Most people attend funerals rarely and, unlike undertakers, health workers and clergy, do not often look death in the face or stand with the bereaved. There is a lot of death on television, both factual and fictional, but we are socially and emotionally distanced from it. Yet in the face of Christ on the cross, we see the knowing suffering of Christ, whose hour has come. For his death is the death of death, and the hope of resurrection for us all.

How can you prepare for your own final hour, spiritually and practically?

GORDON GILES

Holy Saturday

It was the day of Preparation, and the sabbath was beginning. The women who had come with him from Galilee followed, and they saw the tomb and how his body was laid. Then they returned, and prepared spices and ointments. On the sabbath they rested according to the commandment.

Any death is a shock to our system. Time slows and we remember things vividly, forever. On a public level, in reference to a major tragedy, we can often say exactly where we were and what we were doing when it happened. The assassination of President Kennedy (1963), the death of Diana, Princess of Wales (1997), and the destruction of the Twin Towers (2001) are such pivotal events. The more personally affecting death of a loved one has the same effect.

The women who waited at the cross did not leave, but saw Joseph of Arimathea ask Pilate for Jesus' body and made a mental note of where he buried him. Alongside the emotional paralysis of grief is the need to be practical. When someone dies there is a lot to do. When my brother died suddenly in Spain, I had to organise a flight, get there, meet my nephew, visit the undertakers, fill in the legal forms (in Spanish), identify him, organise a small funeral, pay the bill, conduct the funeral, identify him again and sign a form at the point of cremation, speak to his landlord, collect his ashes, deal with the airline and airport security, and fly home to give his mortal remains to my parents. I had just three days. How practical one can be in the face of necessity! Mine is not an extreme example, since in many cultures, first-century Palestine included, death is dealt with deftly, and it is perhaps only after the formalities have been conducted according to the commandments of the time that reality and sorrow sink in.

I remember it vividly. Memory is on dual duty: memories which form because of the significance of what is happening, and the practical, administrative things one has to remember, which, for the women who followed Jesus to his grave, included noting where it was so that they could return the next day to fulfil the law.

What do you need to remember about the death of Jesus?

GORDON GILES

Easter Day

On the first day of the week, at early dawn, they came to the tomb, taking the spices that they had prepared. They found the stone rolled away from the tomb, but when they went in, they did not find the body. While they were perplexed about this, suddenly two men in dazzling clothes stood beside them.

The women have remembered where the tomb is because when Jesus died they were able to both grieve and be practical at the same time. Yet something was about to happen which they could never forget, and which 2,000 years of history and billions of people have remembered with unique joy ever since.

There is no event in your life or mine that compares with what the women experienced on Easter morning. No doubt we can each remember moments of great joy, pain or even both. Childbirth, marriage, bad news, good news, winning a prize, passing exams or a test, getting a job, moments of pride in oneself or others, times of great terror or tragedy. Roll all of that into one and merely approximate what happened on Easter Day! None of us has ever experienced the resurrection of anyone at first hand, nor ever will. Very few have lost a loved one's body.

These women go to do what is normal when someone dies. People die every day, and in Roman-occupied Jerusalem the execution of criminals was not uncommon. Because they had forgotten Jesus' words (as we shall see tomorrow), they had no inkling of what they were to encounter. The shock must have been massive. No wonder they were perplexed and forgot things Jesus said. Rather, they remembered the practical things, being in a daze: the autopilot that drives us through the early stages of bereavement.

It is very easy to be on autopilot through Easter and Holy Week. The story does not change, so it is easy not to pay attention. In recent years, however, the scenery has been different, and perhaps this year it will be different again. But it might not. Either way, let us really try to notice Easter.

Remember last Easter? Where were you? What did you do? Give thanks for this year and hold before God all who have died, in resurrection hope.

GORDON GILES

Easter Monday

The men said to them, 'Why do you look for the living among the dead? He is not here, but has risen. Remember how he told you, while he was still in Galilee, that the Son of Man must be handed over to sinners, and be crucified, and on the third day rise again.' Then they remembered his words.

There are many angels in the Bible. Gabriel visits Mary and Joseph. Angels minister to Jesus after his temptations. Archangel Michael defeats Satan. Yet whatever we think of angelic intervention, they are actually messengers. Just as they declared 'Glory in the highest' to the Bethlehem shepherds at Christ's birth, here an angel gives good news to the women at his tomb. It may not seem good at first, but the angel guarding the tomb gives a message of remembrance that is the first key in the unlocking of the mystery of resurrection. It takes the disciples a few hours and days to see the light, but this angel points them and us in the right direction. And the angel does so by telling them to remember. Without remembering, the re-membering of the risen Christ makes no sense. Which is to say that nothing 'clicks' without a reminder of past prophecies, which unlock the present moment and reveal a fantastic future. In the midst of grief and surprise, they need this jolt from the reminding angel, the messenger of God.

Many things in life make no sense without reference to the past. This can be the great sadness of dementia or other forms of memory loss. Without a past we barely exist. If one cannot remember that someone has been pregnant for nine months, the arrival of a baby is very confusing. A memory can unlock an experience, and so memory loss can lock someone out of their own mental home. This is painful and distressing for everyone concerned. Yet it can happen to any of us if under stress or strain. It is so easy to forget something that seemed irrelevant or trivial at the time, as the disciples did, but which turns out to be hugely significant. Remembering that Jesus predicted what would happen turns unbearable grief into hope and joy. The key is the good news – 'Christ is risen.'

What do you need to unlock your faith?
Remember Easter joys of times past.

GORDON GILES

Easter Tuesday

Now it was Mary Magdalene, Joanna, Mary the mother of James, and the other women with them who told this to the apostles. But these words seemed to them an idle tale, and they did not believe them. But Peter got up and ran to the tomb; stooping and looking in, he saw the linen cloths by themselves.

Have you ever been told something you did not believe but which you later found out was true? Maybe some of our experiences of and reactions to coronavirus situations have been a bit like this, as we have been forced to come to terms with unbelievable, unreal, painful realities, personally and nationally. In 2020–21 we followed the news in agonised disbelief as thousands died and the country ground to a halt. Perhaps we did not believe it because we did not want to believe it. Like the comedy character Victor Meldrew, we can sometimes exclaim 'I don't believe it' not because we don't believe something, but precisely because we do. To say that you 'do not believe' something is sometimes more of a resentful acceptance than a rejection.

In the upper room, where the disciples are hiding when the women tell them that Jesus' body is gone, the disciples, perhaps including Thomas, do not want to believe what they are being told. In their culture, the testimony of women was easier to dismiss. Bereaved, frightened, resentful, the disciples do not want any more bad news, so they refuse to believe it, dismissing it in whatever way they can.

Peter does not behave like this. Perhaps he wants to believe it. Guilt-ridden, perhaps he does believe it. Remembering his failing in denying Jesus, perhaps he senses a chance to be redeemed of it. Perhaps it is true. Perhaps. He does not delay but rushes out. It is not just that he believes the women when others do not, it is also that he wants it to be true, and something in his memory gives his desire a sufficiently hopeful dimension as to make him waste no time in finding out for himself.

Belief in Jesus' resurrection is something that many dismiss as idle talk. Is it?

GORDON GILES

Easter Wednesday

Now on that same day two of them were going to a village called Emmaus, about seven miles from Jerusalem, and talking with each other about all these things that had happened. While they were talking and discussing, Jesus himself came near and went with them, but their eyes were kept from recognising him.

When something striking happens, it is natural to 'go over it' in one's mind and to discuss it with others. It's good to talk. Talking something through, revisiting an experience with another person, helps us come to terms with an experience, to cement it in memory and understanding. When someone dies, it can be very hard for the bereaved to talk about it, because to discuss it is to be forced to admit the reality of it. This is why it can be so hard to break the news of someone's death. Being able to say it is the first hurdle in coming to terms with it.

This part of the Emmaus journey reveals one of its most human aspects: the two disciples are 'going over' what has happened. They are retelling a story that they each know and to which they have both been party, and in doing so they are coming to terms with what seems so unbelievable. Saying it out loud helps. So does the fact that they are walking. For the journey is a mental one too. As they walk, they move forward in understanding and belief, traversing a mental distance of comprehension. Without undermining the reality of the journey they take, there is also a journey of understanding echoed in the passage, as they travel not only physically from Jerusalem to Emmaus (seven miles), but also spiritually and emotionally from disbelief to faith, as ultimately Jesus breaks bread and they realise the meaning of what has happened.

This is a journey we all need to take, as we 'go over' the Easter events mentally and spiritually, in order to come to terms with them, relating them to our lives and owning the risen Christ in our own bodies and souls. In this way we truly re-member the death and resurrection of Jesus in ourselves and our lives.

Which aspects of the Easter story do you need to re-member in your own heart and mind?

GORDON GILES

Easter Thursday

When he was at the table with them, he took bread, blessed and broke it, and gave it to them. Then their eyes were opened, and they recognised him; and he vanished from their sight. They said to each other, 'Were not our hearts burning within us while he was talking to us on the road, while he was opening the scriptures to us?'

This 'pub supper' was the first Holy Communion. At the last supper, Jesus said to 'do this in remembrance of me', breaking bread and giving wine. Then in that Emmaus inn Jesus did it himself. We saw how Proust invested a madeleine with an associative power that drove remembrance (see 12 April); here Jesus does it with his own distinctive, familiar gesture. He shows them and us that he is recognisable in the bread, by actually doing it himself. Re-membered among them as the companion on the road, he helps them recognise and remember uniquely. The word 'companion' means 'the one with whom one eats bread'. But this is no ordinary bread, but the bread of remembering, the bread of re-membering as the risen Christ becomes a reality to and among them. The church has been doing it ever since.

As well as sacramental remembering in this encounter, there is also the word. Jesus, the Word made flesh, 'opens the scriptures' to his companions, explaining the 'Old' Testament in such a way that it takes on new meaning and new purpose. The church has also been doing this ever since. Jesus was the first person to teach anyone how to see the presence of Christ in texts that predate him. No wonder they remembered and told their friend Luke! All scripture involves memory. The most ancient of texts have been remembered by generations long before they could be read. At the beginning of his gospel Luke says that he is collecting those remembrances and setting them down.

The sacrament of bread and wine is spiritual: a living power of re-remembering as the bread becomes body, taken into the bodies of those who are the body of Christ here and now. The word of scripture is set down, a collection of recorded written remembrances.

Christ has no body on earth but ours. Let us remember that.

GORDON GILES

Easter Friday

'A ghost does not have flesh and bones as you see that I have'… He showed them his hands and his feet. While in their joy they were disbelieving… he said… 'Have you anything here to eat?' They gave him a piece of broiled fish, and he took it and ate in their presence.

Have you ever had a sense of déjà vu ('already seen') when something seems to have happened before exactly as it is happening now? It feels like our memory is playing games with us as the past and present become blurred.

It is not what Jesus ate, but the fact that he ate which is important here. It was a pivotal moment of revealing, and we can imagine the disciples saying to Luke, 'We remember Jesus eating after the resurrection. We even remember what he ate!' The fish adds authenticity to the remarkable claim that the risen Christ ate a meal. This means he could not have been conjured up from imagination or the underworld. Nor was it déjà vu. Rather it was a memorable moment which Luke has given us for the benefit of any doubt. The resurrection is not a conjuring trick, nor simply a spiritual nicety, but a physical event involving human flesh eating fishy flesh.

This physicality of the resurrection does not undermine its spiritual significance. We know what hunger is, and many go hungry too often. Food is a physical necessity. There are spiritual necessities too. Jesus was born in a manger, and Luke tells those birth stories, complete with Bethlehem shepherds and angels. Bethlehem means 'house of bread', and a manger is a feeding trough. Jesus, the bread of life who by an act of remembrance makes his body the food of Holy Communion, himself eats fish. It was likely the same kind of fish (sardines) that are caught in the Galilee lake, five of which a boy contributed to the impromptu banquet when Jesus fed 5,000 souls. As well as a very earthly, literal dimension to the eating of fish on the beach after the resurrection, there is a sense of déjà vu as memorable events are interwoven in an eternal braid.

Are there times when God has guided you into awareness or action by weaving strands of your life together?

GORDON GILES

Easter Saturday

Then he led them out as far as Bethany, and, lifting up his hands, he blessed them. While he was blessing them, he withdrew from them and was carried up into heaven. And they worshipped him, and returned to Jerusalem with great joy.

Farewells are memorable. Whether dropping off one's child at school, waving goodbye on a platform or the deathbed 'I love you', these moments stay with us. They are powerful because everything invested in the relationship so far is somehow bound up in them. And whatever the future holds begins now. Anyone who lost a loved one to Covid-19, unable to say final goodbyes, knows the pain of not having that farewell moment.

Many people would rather have the sweet sorrow of parting than be denied it. For in saying 'farewell', be it forever or briefly, we seek to offer and receive a kind of blessing. Next time you say goodbye to someone, reflect on what you mean and how it relates to the past, present and future.

When I moved from a parish in Enfield to Rochester Cathedral in 2020, lockdown restrictions prevented any kind of send-off or farewell. It is hard to disentangle whether the pain of not being able to 'leave properly' is worse than the sadness of leaving itself. It was surreal, unnatural, as after 17 years as vicar, we quietly moved out, unwaved.

The disciples noticed and remembered Jesus' final blessing, which contrasted with the farewell from the cross, when he expired with words of forgiveness and commendation to God. The emotional dynamic of the ascension is the opposite of the cross. Instead of agony and despair, there is peace and hope. The disciples leave rejoicing, reconciled to all that has happened and will happen. It is a special moment of fond farewell and Christian commission.

So it is right now. Having peered through mists of memory at Jesus leaving our apostolic ancestors, we think of our goodbyes, said and unsaid, and anticipate those yet to come. And, after two weeks together on the roads to the cross, to Emmaus, to the beach and now to Bethany, here we part company. Farewell, my friends.

God be with you till we meet again.

GORDON GILES

Acts 16—20

Some of my favourite books as a child were those written by Geoffrey Willans and illustrated by Ronald Searle about an English prep school – St Custard's. Purporting to be guides to 'skool life for tiny pupils and their parents', written by a young boarder, Nigel Molesworth, they have merits too many to mention. One part that particularly sticks in my mind, however, is Nigel's decision to keep a diary. To begin with, his entries are copious and detailed, but they soon become shorter until the day's entry becomes merely 'forget what did', whereupon Nigel decides not to keep one any more.

In a way, these four chapters of Acts could be a 'forget what did' account of Paul's travels through Macedonia to Corinth. He works, he preaches, he baptises, he moves on – it is difficult to distinguish the stories from each other. But this would be to do a grave disservice to the incredible impact of Paul's missionary journeys on the individuals who encountered him. Paul is happy to speak to hundreds of people in the open air of the marketplace or tens of worshippers in the synagogue, but he is equally happy to spend time with the women by the river or the jailer guarding the prisoners. Ordinary people doing everyday tasks encounter the risen Christ through Paul, and their lives are changed. New communities are formed, new ways of living are explored and churches are founded and grown. And all for the glory of God and the growth of his kingdom, in humble recognition that without God's grace nothing would be achieved.

We may not have the gifts of Paul – not many people do. But we can each of us have a significant impact on the communities in which we live. No day should be a 'forget what did' day; every day is filled with opportunities for sharing God's love with those we encounter, whether through kind words, generous deeds or supportive actions.

Teach me, my God and King,
in all things thee to see,
and what I do in anything
to do it as for thee.
(George Herbert, 1593–1633)

SALLY WELCH

No one special?

On the sabbath day we went outside the gate by the river, where we supposed there was a place of prayer; and we sat down and spoke to the women who had gathered there. A certain woman named Lydia, a worshipper of God, was listening to us; she was from the city of Thyatira and a dealer in purple cloth. The Lord opened her heart to listen eagerly to what was said by Paul. When she and her household were baptised, she urged us, saying, 'If you have judged me to be faithful to the Lord, come and stay at my home.' And she prevailed upon us.

Following a vision in which 'a man from Macedonia' has called him, Paul has arrived at Philippi, a leading city of the district. As a Christian who is also a Jew, Paul would have looked for a synagogue, but Philippi being largely settled by former Roman soldiers and their families, he found none. So he went to the river, a traditional place of prayer.

We could read what happens next as just another conversion and baptism, as Paul meets Lydia, a Gentile, who is yet a 'worshipper of God'. Lydia's heart is opened and, following her baptism, Paul stays with her while he is in Philippi. So far, so nothing special. And yet her life is transformed. She becomes part of the Christian community, and when Paul finally leaves Philippi, he stops by her house to say goodbye to Lydia and the 'brothers and sisters' who have gathered there.

So, person by person, the transforming work of the Lord goes on. We might wish for mass conversions and huge waves of revival, but in the story of the kingdom, everybody counts. Because of Lydia, Paul finds a place to call home for a while. Because of Lydia, a new Christian community is supported and nurtured. Because of Lydia, the light of God's love can shine in yet another corner of the world.

Let us not underestimate the small steps we take every day – steps of faith, gestures of loving kindness, offers of hospitality. For each step takes us further along the path to eternity.

'Every journey starts with a single step.' What step can you make today?

SALLY WELCH

I believe!

When the jailer woke up and saw the prison doors wide open, he drew his sword and was about to kill himself, since he supposed that the prisoners had escaped. But Paul shouted in a loud voice, 'Do not harm yourself, for we are all here.' The jailer called for lights, and rushing in, he fell down trembling before Paul and Silas. Then he brought them outside and said, 'Sirs, what must I do to be saved?' They answered, 'Believe on the Lord Jesus, and you will be saved, you and your household.' They spoke the word of the Lord to him and to all who were in his house. At the same hour of the night he took them and washed their wounds; then he and his entire family were baptised without delay.

What a dramatic story this is! All the essential elements that are required for a real page-turner – huge natural disaster, stomach-churning fear, point-of-death scenario, surprise ending. And in the midst of it all, Paul and Silas, calm and fearless, facing death unafraid. Even in the midst of the noise and confusion, they still put first things first – their role is not to escape but to share the good news of the gospel. They take advantage of the situation not for their own good but for that of their jailer, reaching out to him in his moment of fear to offer both earthly and eternal life as free gifts. He washes their wounds and heals them; they baptise him and heal him in turn.

What can we learn from this? That miracles happen, perhaps; that fear can be overcome; that always, everywhere, there is an opportunity to share the good news of the gospel with those around us and that we should not be afraid to make the most of it. Or perhaps we simply repeat to ourselves 'Believe on the Lord Jesus and you will be saved', taking comfort from its simplicity of action and, if necessary, repeating that heartfelt prayer of a father seeking a miracle for his son, 'I believe; help my unbelief!' (Mark 9:24).

I believe it, I believe it,
Jesus died to set me free.
On the cross he bought my pardon,
Hallelujah, he saves me.
(Charles Tindley, 1851–1933)

SALLY WELCH

In the marketplace

Then Paul stood in front of the Areopagus and said, 'Athenians, I see how extremely religious you are in every way. For as I went through the city and looked carefully at the objects of your worship, I found among them an altar with the inscription, "To an unknown god." What therefore you worship as unknown, this I proclaim to you. The God who made the world and everything in it, he who is Lord of heaven and earth, does not live in shrines made by human hands, nor is he served by human hands, as though he needed anything, since he himself gives to all mortals life and breath and all things.'

The Areopagus was both a place and an institution. It is a hill situated next to the Acropolis in Athens, but it was also the name for the court of justice that met there. So Paul, in choosing the site for his famous speech, has found the cultural, historical, political and social heart of the city. He hasn't begun in the synagogues, where he might at least find people who are familiar with the God of the Torah, but has plunged right in among the temples and statues dedicated to the multitude of gods to whom the Athenians gave their loyalty. Jesus, too, although he worshipped in synagogues and on occasion spoke in them, spent his time outside institutions, in the marketplaces, beside wells, in the fields, on the road.

We are all charged with the same task as Paul – that of sharing the good news of God's love to all people and of Jesus' redeeming action on the cross. We can do that in ways which are as many and different as we are ourselves, but one thing is certain – we cannot confine ourselves to the cosy familiarity of the church. What we have been given is so precious that we cannot keep it to ourselves, and so we too must go into the marketplaces and the fields of today, sharing our faith as best we can.

Heavenly Father, give me the courage to step beyond the familiar and comfortable and to share your love with those around me, in whatever way I can.

SALLY WELCH

Your own poets

'From one ancestor he made all nations to inhabit the whole earth, and he allotted the times of their existence and the boundaries of the places where they would live, so that they would search for God and perhaps grope for him and find him – though indeed he is not far from each one of us. For "In him we live and move and have our being"; as even some of your own poets have said, "For we too are his offspring."'

You have to admire Paul – here again he shows just what a marvellous evangelist he is. With great subtlety he moves his audience from what they know and are familiar with to considering and exploring a new and different interpretation of the universe. He quotes directly from their poets – he shows not only that he is aware of their culture but that he is in tune with it and appreciates it. And then, in a masterful way, he demonstrates how the Christian God is not only perfectly compatible with Athenian culture, but that he is in fact its founder and creator.

We don't all have the oratorical skills of Paul – we cannot all argue so skilfully and with such conviction that great numbers are persuaded to become Christian. What we can do is refuse to live in a Christian 'bubble' and instead engage constantly with the 'secular' world, showing how everything that is created is part of God's plan and that he can be found everywhere, not just within the confines of the church building or community.

It is in our nature to seek after God – we do not always realise that 'he is not far from each one of us'. One of our roles is to demonstrate God's nearness to all people, in all things, crossing every boundary. How we do this is up to us, but being alongside our fellow 'Athenians', engaging with their culture but showing God's action within it, is a good way to begin.

For the love of God is broader
Than the measures of the mind;
And the heart of the Eternal
Is most wonderfully kind.
(Frederick Faber, 1814–63)

SALLY WELCH

Do not be afraid

One night the Lord said to Paul in a vision, 'Do not be afraid, but speak and do not be silent; for I am with you, and no one will lay a hand on you to harm you, for there are many in this city who are my people.' He stayed there for a year and six months, teaching the word of God among them.

Paul departed from Athens and made for Corinth. He lodged with Aquila and Priscilla, earning his keep as a day labourer, working at his trade of tent-maker. He spoke earnestly and at great length in the synagogues, trying to persuade the Jewish people that Christ was indeed the longed-for Messiah, but without success. So he has moved his efforts to the Gentiles. He no longer preaches in the synagogue, but instead works from the house of Titius Justus, a 'worshipper of God'. It is when he is engaged upon this work that he hears the Lord speak to him in a vision.

What interests and encourages me is not that the Lord speaks to Paul. He has done that before; Paul is clearly a channel for God's work and very receptive to his word. It is not the fact that God spoke, but that he found it necessary to do so. Paul, the champion evangelist, establishing churches wherever he goes, converting hundreds of households: that same Paul is afraid and discouraged. He has been mentally and emotionally battered by the Jewish people in Corinth, who have aggressively and abusively opposed his words of love and hope, and it has hit him hard.

So God speaks. 'Do not be afraid,' he says, as he has said so many times before, to so many people – 'Do not be afraid, Abraham, Joseph, Moses, David, Zechariah, Mary, Peter, all you my children, for I am with you.'

Through his words to Paul, God reminds us of his constant, loving presence, and he encourages us to keep going as we struggle and dream and try to live our lives in fulfilment of his purposes for all of us – you, me and even Paul.

'Do not let your hearts be troubled, and do not let them be afraid'
(John 14:27).

SALLY WELCH

Crunch time

About that time no little disturbance broke out concerning the Way. A man named Demetrius, a silversmith who made silver shrines of Artemis, brought no little business to the artisans. These he gathered together, with the workers of the same trade, and said, 'Men, you know that we get our wealth from this business. You also see and hear that not only in Ephesus but in almost the whole of Asia this Paul has persuaded and drawn away a considerable number of people by saying that gods made with hands are not gods. And there is danger not only that this trade of ours may come into disrepute but also that the temple of the great goddess Artemis will be scorned, and she will be deprived of her majesty that brought all Asia and the world to worship her.'

Well, this is where the rubber meets the road, as the saying goes. A small group of people have heard Paul and his companions preach, and they are convinced that Jesus Christ is Lord. But how committed are they? Are they really prepared to give everything up for Christ?

Just as the rich man was challenged by Jesus to sell everything he has and give the money to the poor (Mark 10:21), so these silversmiths are being given a choice. And it's not an easy one – stay in business by making statues of false gods or place all your hopes in 'treasure in heaven'. To make things worse, Demetrius, the man in charge of silversmithing commissions, drops in little seeds of doubt by threatening the workers with the anger of Artemis. So the question becomes not just 'What if I have to wait until heaven?', but also 'What if there isn't even any treasure in heaven?'

In our lives we will have similar choices – do we do the Christian thing or the expedient one? Do we turn the other cheek or satisfy our need for revenge? Do we make sacrifices for the poor or spend our hard-earned wealth on ourselves? We will make wrong choices, undoubtedly. But we will also make right ones, and little by little journey nearer towards the kingdom.

'Choose this day whom you will serve' (Joshua 24:15).

SALLY WELCH

The gift of grace, the grace of giving

'And now I commend you to God and to the message of his grace, a message that is able to build you up and to give you the inheritance among all who are sanctified. I coveted no one's silver or gold or clothing. You know for yourselves that I worked with my own hands to support myself and my companions. In all this I have given you an example that by such work we must support the weak, remembering the words of the Lord Jesus, for he himself said, "It is more blessed to give than to receive."'

A family I know has a daughter who suffers from bouts of depression. They have tried to help in all sorts of ways, but none so far have helped her to avoid sinking into what she describes as a 'black bog under a dark cloud'. She cannot always tell what the triggers will be, but the family has learnt to recognise the warning signs. When these appear, they gather round her to support, protect, encourage and nurture her. It is a beautiful thing to witness, despite its terrible necessity. The family has stayed strong and close – there is a mutual agreement to continue to offer all necessary help for as long as it is needed.

When we use the phrase 'It is more blessed to give than to receive', we tend to think in terms of 'silver or gold or clothing'. In a way, such material things are easier to give to someone than time, attention, patience or understanding. They are transactional, and the transaction is speedily concluded. But 'supporting the weak' takes many forms. It might well be that this involves donating money or goods to charities, but there is more. We can listen patiently to the lonely neighbour as they tell us the same story for the third time. We can take over an irksome task so that others can have a break. We can offer friendly support to those who are overwhelmed by life. By allowing the message of God's grace to build us up, we can offer that grace to those around us, so that they too can receive 'the inheritance'.

'Tis grace hath brought me safe thus far, and grace will lead me home'
(John Newton, 1725–1807).

SALLY WELCH

Become a Friend of BRF
and give regularly
to support our ministry

We help people of all ages to grow in faith

We encourage and support individual Christians and churches as they serve and resource the changing spiritual needs of communities today.

Through **Anna Chaplaincy** we're enabling churches to provide spiritual care to older people

Through **Living Faith** we're nurturing faith and resourcing life-long discipleship

Through **Messy Church** we're helping churches to reach out to families

Through **Parenting for Faith** we're supporting parents as they raise their children in the Christian faith

Our ministry is only possible because of the generous support of individuals, churches, trusts and gifts in wills.

As we look to the future and make plans, **regular donations make a huge difference** in ensuring we can both start and finish projects well.

By becoming a Friend of BRF and giving regularly to our ministry you are partnering with us in the gospel and helping change lives.

How your gift makes a difference

£2 a month — Helps us to develop **Living Faith** resources to use in care homes and communities

£10 a month — Helps us to support churches running the **Parenting for Faith** course and stand alongside parents

£5 a month — Helps us to support **Messy Church** volunteers and resource and grow the wider network

£20 a month — Helps us to resource **Anna Chaplaincy** and improve spiritual care for older people

 How to become a Friend of BRF

Set up a Direct Debit donation at **brf.org.uk/donate** or find out how to set up a Standing Order at **brf.org.uk/friends**

Contact the fundraising team

Email: **giving@brf.org.uk**
Tel: +44 (0)1235 462305
Post: Fundraising team, BRF, 15 The Chambers, Vineyard, Abingdon OX14 3FE

Good to know

If you have any questions, or if you want to change your regular donation or stop giving in the future, do get in touch.

Registered with

FUNDRAISING **REGULATOR**

I would like to make a donation to support BRF.
Please use my gift for:

☐ Where it is most needed ☐ Anna Chaplaincy ☐ Living Faith

☐ Messy Church ☐ Parenting for Faith

Title	First name/initials	Surname

Address

	Postcode

Email

Telephone

Signature	Date

Our ministry is only possible because of the generous support of individuals, churches, trusts and gifts in wills.

giftaid it You can add an extra 25p to every £1 you give.

Please treat as Gift Aid donations all qualifying gifts of money made

☐ today, ☐ in the past four years, ☐ and in the future.

I am a UK taxpayer and understand that if I pay less Income Tax and/or Capital Gains Tax in the current tax year than the amount of Gift Aid claimed on all my donations, it is my responsibility to pay any difference.

☐ My donation does not qualify for Gift Aid.

Please notify BRF if you want to cancel this Gift Aid declaration, change your name or home address, or no longer pay sufficient tax on your income and/or capital gains.

Please complete other side of form ➡

SHARING OUR VISION – MAKING A ONE-OFF GIFT

Please accept my gift of:

☐ £2 ☐ £5 ☐ £10 ☐ £20 Other £ ⬚

by (*delete as appropriate*):

☐ Cheque/Charity Voucher payable to 'BRF'

☐ MasterCard/Visa/Debit card/Charity card

Name on card

Card no. ☐☐☐☐ ☐☐☐☐ ☐☐☐☐ ☐☐☐☐

Expires end ☐☐☐☐ M M Y Y Security code* ☐☐☐

*Last 3 digits on the reverse of the card
ESSENTIAL IN ORDER TO PROCESS
YOUR PAYMENT

Signature ⋮ Date

☐ I would like to leave a gift to BRF in my will.
Please send me further information.

For help or advice regarding making a gift, please contact our fundraising team +44 (0)1865 462305

Your privacy

We will use your personal data to process this transaction. From time to time we may send you information about the work of BRF that we think may be of interest to you. Our privacy policy is available at **brf.org.uk/privacy**. Please contact us if you wish to discuss your mailing preferences.

Registered with

FUNDRAISING
REGULATOR

 Please complete other side of form

Please return this form to 'Freepost BRF'
No other address information or stamp is needed

Bible Reading Fellowship is a charity (233280) and company limited by guarantee (301324), registered in England and Wales

Overleaf... Reading *New Daylight* in a group | Author profile | Recommended reading | Order and subscription forms

Reading *New Daylight* in a group

SALLY WELCH

I am aware that although some of you cherish the moments of quiet during the day which enable you to read and reflect on the passages we offer you in *New Daylight*, other readers prefer to study in small groups, to enable conversation and discussion and the sharing of insights. With this in mind, here are some ideas for discussion starters within a study group. Some of the questions are generic and can be applied to any set of contributions within this issue; others are specific to certain sets of readings. I hope they generate some interesting reflections and conversations!

General discussion starters

These can be used for any study series within this issue. Remember there are no right or wrong answers – these questions are simply to enable a group to engage in conversation.

- What do you think the main idea or theme of the author in this series? Do you think they succeeded in communicating this to you, or were you more interested in the side issues?

- Have you had any experience of the issues that are raised in the study? How have they affected your life?

- What evidence does the author use to support their ideas? Do they use personal observations and experience, facts, quotations from other authorities? Which appeals to you most?

- Does the author make a 'call to action'? Is that call realistic and achievable? Do you think their ideas will work in the secular world?

- Can you identify specific passages that struck you personally – as interesting, profound, difficult to understand or illuminating?

- Did you learn something new reading this series? Will you think differently about some things, and if so, what are they?

Questions for specific series

Looking back (Sally Welch)

What are the benefits and disadvantages of 'looking back'? Which do you prefer to do – look forward or back? How does this affect your spiritual life?

Psalms 71—84 (Paul Gravelle)

Paul writes honestly about the ways in which he finds the Psalms challenging. In what ways do they challenge you?

With reference to Psalm 83, Paul writes: 'Some of the psalms' cursing verses might be a good way to put the fear of God into our demonic enemies.' What is your view on 'spiritual warfare'? How do you combat spiritual evil?

Ecclesiastes: enjoying life with God in the real world (Fiona Stratta)

'Meaningless, meaningless', writes the author of Ecclesiastes. Fiona describes the book as 'the truth written plainly'. Does the author's view of life match yours? In which ways do they differ?

'The dust returns to the ground it came from, and the spirit returns to God who gave it' (Ecclesiastes 12:7, NIV). How easy do you find it to think of death, particularly your own? Do the insights of these reflections help at all?

1 and 2 Thessalonians (Liz Hoare)

'For we know, brothers and sisters beloved by God, that he has chosen you' (1 Thessalonians 1:4, NRSV). In what ways do you feel chosen by God? How does this affect the way you speak and act?

Paul encourages his readers to imitate him. What habits of yours are worth imitating? What habits of others whom you know?

How often do you pray for your church leaders – and what do you pray for?

Remembering Holy Week and Easter (Gordon Giles)

Gordon Giles writes that 'it is very easy to be on autopilot through Holy Week and Easter', because the story is so familiar to us. Read the Easter story in Luke as if you were reading it for the first time. Read it slowly and carefully, imagining every scene. What impressions do you get? What do you notice? Which parts of the action resonate with you right now?

Meet the author: Gordon Giles

Can you briefly share some highlights of your faith journey with us?
I was baptised the day I was born because I was not expected to live! As a music student I was involved in the chaplaincy at Lancaster University, where I felt a calling to ordained ministry, and after a year working for the Missions to Seafarers I studied for the ministry at Ridley Hall. I served my curacy in Cambridge, before moving to St Paul's Cathedral as succentor, where it was a joy to be immersed in, and to some extent responsible for, the rich musical spiritual life of St Paul's. I then served in Enfield for 17 years, loving the diverse pattern of pastoral, community, preaching, teaching and liturgical ministry there.

Who has been your greatest spiritual influence?
Friends and colleagues over the years have taught me greatly and influenced me deeply; it is through many conversations as well as through prayer and reading that I have nourished my faith. Theologically I admire the thinking of Karl Barth, not only in terms of doctrine and ethics, but also for the idea that faith is not an aspect of our lives, but faith *is* our life.

You moved from a parish situation to a cathedral – what are the similarities and differences in ministry between the two?
In a cathedral the clergy are in the minority, as there are invariably more staff than clergy. There is more of an office culture, and it is not to be gainsaid that everyone who works in a cathedral has a strong Christian faith. Parishes rely heavily on volunteers to do jobs that in the context of a cathedral are done by paid staff. It's not better or worse, just different. In a parish the vicar can be left to do all sorts of things without assistance, whereas cathedrals are thoroughly collaborative environments. Similarly some of the issues that affect major tourist venues have also kicked in – worship is not the only thing that goes on within cathedrals, although they still have congregations to minister to, so it is, in the classic sense of the phrase, the same but different!

What sets your soul alight?
I love church music, and especially hymnody. I love to sing and choral worship is where I find my spiritual home. Thus, it is a joy to return to cathedral ministry.

Recommended reading

In this year's BRF Lent book Sally Welch explores two questions: what is the Easter story really about, and how do we share it? Through each week of Lent, a different aspect of the Easter story is examined: repenting, changing, hoping, trusting, forgiving, loving and sacrificing. Within each week, the days are focused on what we need to do in order to share the story: listening, understanding, reflecting, living, telling, sharing and becoming. Each day offers a Bible passage, followed by a reflection and prayer activity. Suggestions for group study and group study questions are also included.

One hundred years ago, in 1922, the Fellowship of St Matthew was begun in a church in south London in response to a congregation's eagerness for informed and helpful support in building a habit of daily Bible reading. In 1926, it became known as the Bible Reading Fellowship (BRF) as its influence spread and more and more church communities subscribed to the notes and prayers which were offered.

Today, BRF resources people and groups as they grow in faith, encouraging them to deepen their relationship with God and to share the good news of Jesus Christ with others.

This Lent study book is written in response to BRF's vision of 'Sharing the Story', by looking at the events leading up to Easter. It will take you on a journey through familiar and unfamiliar parts of the Bible, reading and reflecting on our Christian faith.

But first we need to explore what it means to share our story. For me, it begins with *listening* – listening deeply and carefully, to God, to others, to the world and to ourselves. With careful listening will come a greater degree of *understanding*. We will probably never understand everything, but we as we stretch our minds and our hearts, we will progress and grow – and our faith will deepen also.

Once we have listened to the word of God and understood it as far as we are able, we must take time to *reflect* upon it. During difficult and stressful times, I have found it extremely helpful to take a Bible passage and just spend time thinking about what it means. Sometimes the passage brings wisdom for my situation; sometimes it doesn't speak to that at all, but I gain some other insight.

The process of listening, understanding and reflecting leads to us being able to absorb the passage into our hearts. We begin to *live* the biblical wisdom as we seek to act upon its teaching and adjust our lives accordingly. That is the stage at which we might begin to share with others the insights we have gained, when we begin to *tell* others the story of God's saving love for each of us. Once we have told it, the story is *shared* – we become part of a community of storytellers, of good-news givers, of children of the gospel. Then we may *become* the story we reflect upon, live and share.

And what is this story? What are the elements of the last few weeks of Jesus' life, his death and his resurrection which bring hope to the world? We begin by beginning again – by acknowledging our wrongdoing and seeking God's help to turn our lives around to face the direction in which God is moving. Once we have repented, we can forgive and be forgiven, a constantly renewing challenge to give and receive forgiveness. This is achieved because we place our hope in the resurrection – we witness the kingdom breaking through into our lives and the lives of others, and so reinforce our trust in God and in his Son, who will deliver and redeem all those who put their trust in him. We reflect on the sacrifice of God in Christ and learn what it is to live sacrificial lives ourselves, offering prayer and praise through worship and service to the one who gives us grace without asking for anything in return. As we approach the end of Lent and arrive at the glory of Easter, we can journey boldly wherever God leads us, secure in his love and, through that love, able to love ourselves and to offer love to others, putting our faith in the hope of the kingdom and becoming transformed into God's new creations.

You will notice that all the words are in the present participle – they are all active, 'doing' words. This is because the process is a constant one, full of energy and motion. It is my hope that the Bible stories will grip your imagination, encouraging you to think deeply about all they contain. This book does not aim to proscribe, but to invite you to join me on a journey through Lent to Easter, discovering what it means to 'share the story' of our faith.

Sharing the Easter story as an individual

Every week in Lent you will be introduced to a different element of the Easter story, journeying through the story-sharing process. A short Bible passage is followed by a reflection and a prayer, and some questions to help you reflect for yourself on the passage.

You might like to read the passage out loud, slowly and carefully, allowing time to let the words sink in, pausing at the end of each sentence. You might take one sentence or word which stands out for you and learn it by heart, holding it in your thoughts throughout the day, perhaps journaling what it has come to mean for you by the evening time.

At the end of each week there is a suggestion for a creative prayer and further questions, which can be for groups or individuals.

Sharing the Easter story as a group

The readings and reflections in this book have been set out so that a rhythm of daily study and prayer can be established. In this way a habit of daily encounter with God, which will build us up in our faith and encourage us on our journey, can be formed, renewed or reinforced. I have also tried to encourage the habit of theological reflection by including questions to think about at the end of each day's reflection. These questions can be used by individuals, but can also be used when a number of people gather together as a group to reflect on the theme of the week.

The suggested timetable is for meetings to take place during the week after the date of the readings in question, and the questions are therefore arranged so that groups can begin during the week after Ash Wednesday (that is, the week commencing Monday 7 March), looking at the material for Week 1 (2–6 March). The final group meeting is after Easter Sunday and can be held that week or the following week. In this way, we can be encouraged to think about what comes next – the story didn't end at Easter!

The readings and reflections in this book can be used in different ways by all sorts of groups. It can form the basis for a weekly Lent group or provide topics of discussion at Lent lunches or suppers. It can be used as conversation starters for groups that already meet, such as midweek fellowship groups, Mothers' Union meetings or men's breakfasts.

If a new group is beginning, it is a good idea to include refreshments with each meeting – some groups find an evening meal with discussion round the table very popular, while others feel that drinks and biscuits or cake are more appropriate. This kind of hospitality can break down barriers and introduce people to each other in a relaxed way, which in turn will lead to a livelier, more fruitful discussion.

If you are leading or joining a group, remember that everyone will need their own copy of the book well before the beginning of Lent.

To order a copy of this book, please use the order form on page 151 or visit **brfonline.org.uk**.

Deep Calls to Deep

Spiritual formation
in the hard places of life

Tony Horsfall

The Psalms offer honest insights into the reality of life with God, reflecting every human emotion and situation. Through looking at some of the psalms written 'from the depths' we can understand more fully the way God works to form the life of Christ within us during difficult times in life. This will enable us not only to make sense of our own history with God, but also help us to get to know God here and now, and prepare us for what may lie ahead.

Deep Calls to Deep
Spiritual formation in the hard places of life
Tony Horsfall
978 1 80039 066 9 £8.99
brfonline.org.uk

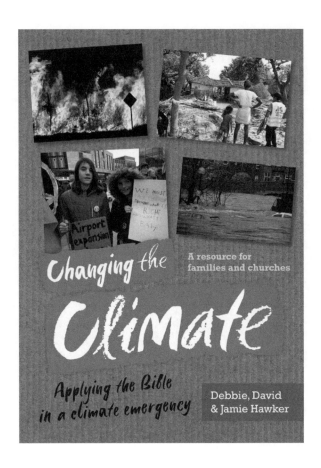

The climate crisis is one of the most important issues of our time, threatening lives and livelihoods. The Bible teaches us that God the creator put humans on the Earth to take care of it; to show love to all, and to care for the poor and vulnerable. This workbook shows how the Bible is relevant to environmentalism, and how we can all play our part in limiting the negative effects of climate change.

Changing the Climate
Applying the Bible in a climate emergency
Debbie, David and Jamie Hawker
978 1 80039 022 5 £9.99
brfonline.org.uk

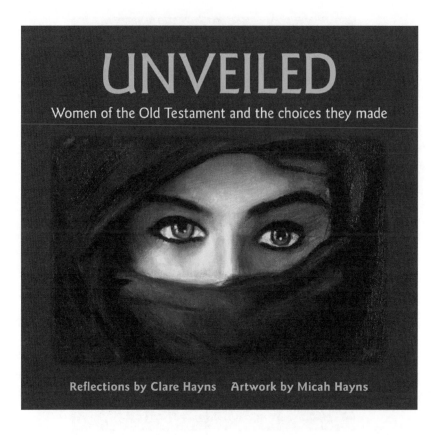

Some women of the Hebrew scriptures are well known, but many others are barely remembered. Even when they are, we often don't pause on them long enough to think about what we might learn from them. *Unveiled*, written with frankness and humour and illustrated with striking artwork from a young Oxford-based artist, explores the stories of 40 women in 40 days. Each reflection ends with a short application to everyday life, guidance for further thought and a prayer.

Unveiled
Women of the Old Testament and the choices they made
Clare Hayns, with artwork by Micah Hayns
978 1 80039 072 0 £9.99
brfonline.org.uk

To order

Online: **brfonline.org.uk**
Telephone: +44 (0)1865 319700
Mon–Fri 9.30–17.00

Delivery times within the UK are normally 15 working days. Prices are correct at the time of going to press but may change without prior notice.

Title	Price	Qty	Total
Sharing the Easter Story	£8.99		
Deep Calls to Deep	£8.99		
Changing the Climate	£9.99		
Unveiled	£9.99		

POSTAGE AND PACKING CHARGES			
Order value	UK	Europe	Rest of world
Under £7.00	£2.00		
£7.00–£29.99	£3.00	Available on request	Available on request
£30.00 and over	FREE		

Total value of books	
Postage and packing	
Donation*	
Total for this order	

* Please complete and return the Gift Aid declaration on page 139.

Please complete in BLOCK CAPITALS

Title _____ First name/initials _____ Surname _____

Address _____

_____ Postcode _____

Acc. No. _____ Telephone _____

Email _____

Method of payment

☐ Cheque (made payable to BRF) ☐ MasterCard / Visa

Card no. ☐☐☐☐ ☐☐☐☐ ☐☐☐☐ ☐☐☐☐ ☐☐☐☐

Expires end ☐☐ ☐☐ Security code ☐☐☐ Last 3 digits on the reverse of the card

Signature _____ Date _____ / _____ / _____

We will use your personal data to process this order. From time to time we may send you information about the work of BRF. Please contact us if you wish to discuss your mailing preferences **brf.org.uk/privacy**

Please return this form to:

BRF, 15 The Chambers, Vineyard, Abingdon OX14 3FE | **enquiries@brf.org.uk**
For terms and cancellation information, please visit **brfonline.org.uk/terms**.

Bible Reading Fellowship is a charity (233280) and company limited by guarantee (301324), registered in England and Wales

BRF needs you!

If you're one of our many thousands of regular *New Daylight* readers, you will know all about the impact that regular Bible reading has on your faith and the value of daily notes to guide, inform and inspire you.

Here are some recent comments from *New Daylight* readers:

'Thank you for all the many inspiring writings that help so much when things are tough.'

'Just right for me – I learned a lot!'

'We looked forward to each day's message as we pondered each passage and comment.'

If you have similarly positive things to say about *New Daylight*, would you be willing to share your experience with others? Perhaps you could give a short talk or write a brief article about why you find *New Daylight* so helpful. You could form a *New Daylight* reading group, perhaps supplying members with their first copy of the notes. Or you could pass on your back copies or give someone a gift subscription. However you do it, the important thing is to find creative ways to put a copy of *New Daylight* into someone else's hands.

It doesn't need to be complicated and we can help with group and bulk-buy discounts.

We can supply further information if you need it and and would love to hear about it if you do find ways to get *New Daylight* into new readers' hands.

For more information:

- Email **enquiries@brf.org.uk**
- Telephone BRF on +44 (0)1865 319700 Mon–Fri 9.30–17.00
- Write to us at BRF, 15 The Chambers, Vineyard, Abingdon OX14 3FE

Enabling all ages to grow in faith

At BRF, we long for people of all ages to grow in faith and understanding of the Bible. That's what all our work as a charity is about.

- Our **Living Faith** range of resources helps Christians go deeper in their understanding of scripture, in prayer and in their walk with God. Our conferences and events bring people together to share this journey, while our Holy Habits resources help whole congregations grow together as disciples of Jesus, living out and sharing their faith.

- We also want to make it easier for local churches to engage effectively in ministry and mission – by helping them bring new families into a growing relationship with God through **Messy Church** or by supporting churches as they nurture the spiritual life of older people through **Anna Chaplaincy**.

- Our **Parenting for Faith** team coaches parents and others to raise God-connected children and teens, and enables churches to fully support them.

Do you share our vision?

Though a significant proportion of BRF's funding is generated through our charitable activities, we are dependent on the generous support of individuals, churches and charitable trusts.

If you share our vision, would you help us to enable even more people of all ages to grow in faith? Your prayers and financial support are vital for the work that we do. You could:

- Support BRF's ministry with a regular donation;
- Support us with a one-off gift;
- Consider leaving a gift to BRF in your will (see page 154);
- Encourage your church to support BRF as part of your church's giving to home mission – perhaps focusing on a specific ministry or programme;
- Most important of all, support BRF with your prayers.

Donate at **brf.org.uk/donate** or use the form on pages 139–40.

By faith and not by sight

Therefore we are always confident and know that as long as we are at home in the body we are away from the Lord. For we live by faith, not by sight.

2 CORINTHIANS 5:6–7 (NIV)

In his second letter to the Corinthians, the apostle Paul talks about the fact that for now we are 'at home in the body' and so we must live by faith, trusting God until such a time as we are with the Lord. This faith in the future, in things yet to come, is a challenge we face as Christians, but it is a hopeful challenge, nonetheless.

At BRF we too look to the future with hope. As we move through our centenary year and look ahead into the next hundred years, one thing is certain: we cannot predict what will happen. But, we can act wisely and trust in God's plan for us, living by faith as we continue to make a difference through our ministries – Anna Chaplaincy, Living Faith, Messy Church and Parenting for Faith.

I'd like to invite you to consider prayerfully whether you can support the future of our work through a gift in your will. If you would like further information about leaving a gift in your will to BRF, please get in touch with us on **01235 462305**, via **giving@brf.org.uk** or visit **brf.org.uk/lastingdifference**.

Your prayers, as ever, are hugely appreciated.

Judith Moore
Fundraising development officer

PS: Please be assured that whatever decision you reach about your will, you don't need to tell us and we won't ask. May God grant you wisdom as you reflect on these things.

Give. Pray. Get involved.
brf.org.uk

NEW DAYLIGHT SUBSCRIPTION RATES

Please note our new subscription rates, current until 30 April 2023:

Individual subscriptions
covering 3 issues for under 5 copies, payable in advance
(including postage & packing):

	UK	Europe	Rest of world
New Daylight	£18.30	£26.25	£30.15
New Daylight 3-year subscription (9 issues) (not available for Deluxe)	£53.55	N/A	N/A
New Daylight Deluxe per set of 3 issues p.a.	£22.50	£32.85	£38.85

Group subscriptions
covering 3 issues for 5 copies or more, sent to one UK address (post free):

New Daylight   £14.55 per set of 3 issues p.a.

New Daylight Deluxe   £18.00 per set of 3 issues p.a.

Please note that the annual billing period for group subscriptions runs from 1 May to 30 April.

Overseas group subscription rates
Available on request. Please email **enquiries@brf.org.uk**.

Copies may also be obtained from Christian bookshops:

New Daylight   £4.85 per copy

New Daylight Deluxe   £6.00 per copy

All our Bible reading notes can be ordered online by visiting **brfonline.org.uk/subscriptions**

New Daylight is also available as an app for Android, iPhone and iPad **brfonline.org.uk/apps**

NEW DAYLIGHT INDIVIDUAL SUBSCRIPTION FORM

All our Bible reading notes can be ordered online by visiting
brfonline.org.uk/subscriptions

Title _____ First name/initials _____ Surname _____

Address _____

_____ Postcode _____

Telephone _____ Email _____

Please send *New Daylight* beginning with the May 2022 / September 2022 / January 2023 issue (*delete as appropriate*):

(*please tick box*)	UK	Europe	Rest of world
New Daylight 1-year subscription	☐ £18.30	☐ £26.25	☐ £30.15
New Daylight 3-year subscription	☐ £53.55	N/A	N/A
New Daylight Deluxe	☐ £22.50	☐ £32.85	☐ £38.85

Optional donation to support the work of BRF £ _____

Total enclosed £ _____ (cheques should be made payable to 'BRF')

Please complete and return the Gift Aid declaration on page 139 to make your donation even more valuable to us.

Please charge my MasterCard / Visa with £ _____

Card no. ☐☐☐☐ ☐☐☐☐ ☐☐☐☐ ☐☐☐☐

Expires end ☐☐☐☐ MM YY   Security code ☐☐   Last 3 digits on the reverse of the card

Signature _____ Date _____/_____/_____

To set up a Direct Debit, please complete the Direct Debit instruction on page 159.

We will use your personal data to process this order. From time to time we may send you information about the work of BRF. Please contact us if you wish to discuss your mailing preferences **brf.org.uk/privacy**

Please return this form with the appropriate payment to:
BRF, 15 The Chambers, Vineyard, Abingdon OX14 3FE
For terms and cancellation information, please visit **brfonline.org.uk/terms**.

Bible Reading Fellowship is a charity (233280) and company limited by guarantee (301324), registered in England and Wales

ND0122

NEW DAYLIGHT GIFT SUBSCRIPTION FORM

☐ I would like to give a gift subscription (please provide both names and addresses):

Title .... First name/initials .... Surname ....

Address ....

.... Postcode ....

Telephone .... Email ....

Gift subscription name ....

Gift subscription address ....

.... Postcode ....

Gift message (20 words max. or include your own gift card):

....

....

Please send *New Daylight* beginning with the May 2022 / September 2022 / January 2023 issue (*delete as appropriate*):

(*please tick box*)	UK	Europe	Rest of world
New Daylight 1-year subscription	☐ £18.30	☐ £26.25	☐ £30.15
New Daylight 3-year subscription	☐ £53.55	N/A	N/A
New Daylight Deluxe	☐ £22.50	☐ £32.85	☐ £38.85

Optional donation to support the work of BRF £ ....

Total enclosed £ .... (cheques should be made payable to 'BRF')

Please complete and return the Gift Aid declaration on page 139 to make your donation even more valuable to us.

Please charge my MasterCard / Visa with £ ....

Card no. ☐☐☐☐ ☐☐☐☐ ☐☐☐☐ ☐☐☐☐

Expires end ☐☐ ☐☐ Security code ☐☐☐ Last 3 digits on the reverse of the card

Signature .... Date ...... / ...... / ......

To set up a Direct Debit, please complete the Direct Debit instruction on page 159.

We will use your personal data to process this order. From time to time we may send you information about the work of BRF. Please contact us if you wish to discuss your mailing preferences **brf.org.uk/privacy**

Please return this form with the appropriate payment to:
BRF, 15 The Chambers, Vineyard, Abingdon OX14 3FE
For terms and cancellation information, please visit **brfonline.org.uk/terms**.

Bible Reading Fellowship is a charity (233280) and company limited by guarantee (301324), registered in England and Wales

You can pay for your annual subscription to our Bible reading notes using Direct Debit. You need only give your bank details once, and the payment is made automatically every year until you cancel it. If you would like to pay by Direct Debit, please use the form opposite, entering your BRF account number under 'Reference number'.

You are fully covered by the Direct Debit Guarantee:

The Direct Debit Guarantee

- This Guarantee is offered by all banks and building societies that accept instructions to pay Direct Debits.

- If there are any changes to the amount, date or frequency of your Direct Debit, Bible Reading Fellowship will notify you 10 working days in advance of your account being debited or as otherwise agreed. If you request Bible Reading Fellowship to collect a payment, confirmation of the amount and date will be given to you at the time of the request.

- If an error is made in the payment of your Direct Debit, by Bible Reading Fellowship or your bank or building society, you are entitled to a full and immediate refund of the amount paid from your bank or building society.

- If you receive a refund you are not entitled to, you must pay it back when Bible Reading Fellowship asks you to.

- You can cancel a Direct Debit at any time by simply contacting your bank or building society. Written confirmation may be required. Please also notify us.

Instruction to your bank or building society to pay by Direct Debit

Please fill in the whole form using a ballpoint pen and return with order form to:

BRF, 15 The Chambers, Vineyard, Abingdon OX14 3FE

Service User Number: | 5 | 5 | 8 | 2 | 2 | 9 |

Name and full postal address of your bank or building society

To: The Manager	Bank/Building Society
Address	
	Postcode

Name(s) of account holder(s)

Branch sort code

| | | – | | | – | | |

Bank/Building Society account number

Reference number

Instruction to your Bank/Building Society

Please pay Bible Reading Fellowship Direct Debits from the account detailed in this instruction, subject to the safeguards assured by the Direct Debit Guarantee. I understand that this instruction may remain with Bible Reading Fellowship and, if so, details will be passed electronically to my bank/building society.

Signature(s)

Banks and Building Societies may not accept Direct Debit instructions for some types of account.

ND0122

Enabling all ages to grow in faith

Anna Chaplaincy

Living Faith

Messy Church

Parenting for Faith

100 years of BRF

2022 is BRF's 100th anniversary! Look out for details of our special new centenary resources, a beautiful centenary rose and an online thanksgiving service that we hope you'll attend. This centenary year we're focusing on sharing the story of BRF, the story of the Bible – and we hope you'll share your stories of faith with us too.

Find out more at **brf.org.uk/centenary**.

To find out more about our work, visit

brf.org.uk

Sharing
the Story
since 1922